The Amazon® Marketplace Dilemma

D0170500

THIS IS A BUY BOX EXPERTS BOOK

PUBLISHED BY BUY BOX EXPERTS

Copyright © 2016 by James Thomson and Joseph Hansen.

www.buyboxexperts.com

Portions of "Vendor Central or Seller Central? 1P vs. 3P Amazon Strategies", published January 25, 2016, reprinted with permission of *Web Retailer*.

Library of Congress Cataloguing-in-Publication Data:
Thomson, James
  The Amazon Marketplace Dilemma: A brand executive's challenge growing sales and maintaining control
James Thomson, Joseph Hansen.
  p. cm.
ISBN 978-0-9984846-0-0 (paperback)
ISBN-10:0-9984846-1-X (ebook Kindle)

Manufactured in the United States of America
Second Edition

*NOTE: This book is not sponsored or endorsed by Amazon.
Amazon® is a registered trademark of Amazon Technologies, Inc.*

Finally, we thank the thousands of sellers with whom we have had the privilege of knowing and sharing experiences of the online seller world – as colleagues, clients, prospects and PROSPER Show attendees. Keep the ideas coming, and questions flowing. Together, the battle is fought each day.

TABLE OF CONTENTS

THE AMAZON MARKETPLACE DILEMMA

Brand executives face two key questions in addressing the Amazon marketplace:

1. Will the brand be sold on the Amazon Marketplace?
2. If yes, then what distribution approach makes most sense for the brand?

As we will discuss throughout the book, the decision regarding whether the brand will be sold on the Amazon marketplace is not always solely within a brand's control. It's better to start with the assumption that any popular brand's products will eventually show up for sale on Amazon, whether the brand wants those products there or not.

The second question is more complex for brand executives. At its core, this question represents a pivotal "fork in the road" that we call the *Amazon Marketplace Dilemma*. That choice is:

Sell <u>TO</u> Amazon
vs.
Sell <u>ON</u> Amazon

Which of these paths a brand chooses — and the distribution strategy it employs in that domain — will determine a brand executive's issues, challenges and priorities.

Either option will impact the brand executive's ability to control their brand strategies (e.g., pricing, brand content, marketing, etc.), to generate profits, and to create a stable cadence for managing activities on the Amazon marketplace channel. In our book, we uncover the many considerations involved in developing and implementing the right Amazon distribution strategy for a given brand.

INTRODUCTION

Since the explosion of online retail sites in the early 2000s, when traffic was primarily obtained through organic or paid search, e-commerce has evolved to include a variety of marketing segments that can prove either highly lucrative or costly, depending on the competitiveness of a company's product category. Brands now use a plethora of methods to drive direct consumer traffic and sales for their products, software, and services, including search engine optimization (SEO), social media campaigns, pay-per-click advertising, email/affiliate marketing and now, online marketplaces.

In January 2016, Amazon CEO Jeff Bezos indicated that:

> *"This year, we pass $100 billion in annual sales and serve 300 million customers."* [1]

In 17 years, the Amazon marketplace had grown from merely book and media distribution into the behemoth of e-commerce – and one of the highest valued companies in the world. Such a market opportunity is hard for most brands to turn down. Yet the processes for identifying and capitalizing on this opportunity are often conducted poorly by those responsible for the brands that they manage.

When Amazon was founded in 1994, its original catalog selection consisted of wholesale books and other forms of media. Within six years, the company had grown to almost $3 billion in annual revenue, and captured the bulk of the online media market.

Then in 2000, Amazon confounded many retail experts by going into competition with itself — by adding competitors' products through its newly created third-party marketplace. Amazon customers could now buy from either Amazon Retail (also known as "First-Party," or

---

[1] Amazon Quarterly Earnings, Q1-2016.

"1P"), or from third-party resellers (also known as "3P," "3P Sellers" or "Marketplace Sellers"). As Amazon added new categories of products to the marketplace, it also added more than two million third-party sellers and three hundred million catalog listings — making it the world's largest marketplace of consumer products.

The expansion of both selection and customers has been critical to Amazon's overall success, but the move to include 3P provided another unique advantage. The customer behavior data yielded by this expansion — including customer search and purchase data — has given Amazon extraordinary, real-time insight into the preferences of its 200+ million[2] customers today. Since Amazon shares little of that SKU-level data with external parties, this has created a nearly insurmountable advantage over most of the national and international brands with whom it does business, and over the millions of third-party sellers who market their products on Amazon today.

And because Amazon is not only an active participant in the Amazon marketplace but also the authority that sets the rules, a brand only has a fair shot at revenues and profits in this playing field if its leadership team has a firm grasp of the rules, mechanics, and implications of the Amazon marketplace.

Any person or company can sell on the third-party Amazon marketplace, and these sellers include brand manufacturers, distributors and resellers. With an estimated two million Amazon Sellers in this marketplace, brands are forced to deal with intense competition, less-than-ideal catalog regulation, and sophisticated product diversion. Neglecting this channel can lead to substantial problems with poor content representing the brand and price erosion.

The skills that brands need to be successful on the Amazon channel are quite different from those needed for success in brick-and-mortar

---

[2] Amazon Quarterly Earnings, Q1-2016.

channels. And although growth on the Amazon channel is potentially greater than in most other online and offline channels, most brands don't understand what it takes to succeed on Amazon.

In this book, we examine the critical levers that each brand must explicitly control to ensure its product is properly represented on Amazon, and is able to generate profitable sales without creating significant problems for other distribution channels and retailers.

We provide you with the necessary tools to thrive in this channel, and an understanding of the pitfalls, gold mines, and ever-present noise that Amazon will throw your way.

Bearing the scars and bruises of our own experiences working both inside and now outside of Amazon with hundreds of brands, we share our knowledge so you can make responsible, clear choices about how to best leverage the Amazon channel for your brand.

Our goal is that every reader take away the necessary insights to make optimal Amazon-related decisions for his or her brand portfolio. Every approach and strategy requires tradeoffs, and the risks and opportunities of the Amazon marketplace will affect each brand differently. But with insight and awareness, you can capitalize on the Amazon channel to bring the right balance of control, efficiency and profits.

BOOK SUMMARY

Chapter 1

If you are a brand executive, an investor in a consumer products company, or a distributor trying to make sense of the Amazon opportunity, you need a clear strategic plan to address the major facets of selling on Amazon.

We will begin by examining the importance of the Amazon channel to owners and executives of brands. We will first review the key objectives owners and senior executives typically have regarding their brands, and then we will examine the two business-critical questions about Amazon any brand owner must be able to answer:

1. What impacts can the Amazon marketplace have on a brand's business-critical objectives?

2. What happens when a brand doesn't have an explicit, comprehensive Amazon strategy?

Because the Amazon marketplace works differently from other channels in which a brand may sell its products, there are often critical misunderstandings about what a brand owner can and cannot influence, and what they can do to control their brand on Amazon. It's important to understand what Amazon controls, and how it does and does not empower brands.

Chapter 2

We address the many options available to a brand for selling on the Amazon marketplace. Each option comes with its own set of issues, benefits and downsides, which should be clearly understood so you can develop the right Amazon strategy for your brand.

The main approaches to selling on Amazon include:

1. The "Do Nothing" Approach: resellers sell without the brand's guidance or participation

2. Selling to Amazon Retail (1P): the brand wholesales to Amazon
3. Selling through multiple authorized third-party resellers (Authorized 3P)
4. Selling through exclusive third-party reseller(s) (Exclusive 3P)
5. Selling as exclusive third-party seller of record (B2C model)
6. Blended 1P/3P approach

While no single distribution approach is ideal for all brands, we explore these options to help create awareness of the different models available. Ultimately, the right choice will come down to a few factors relative to the brand's overall business, and we explore those factors in detail.

Chapter 3

In this chapter, we examine key issues brands should consider when selecting the optimal distribution approach for the Amazon marketplace. We review more than 20 of these key business concerns, in each case examining its relationship with the six distribution approaches outlined in the previous chapter[3].

This objective analysis of the pros and cons of each Amazon strategy as it relates to key business aspects will help your brand decide which tradeoffs are tolerable, and which strategy is best.

Chapter 4

In this chapter, we discuss how you can be proactive in controlling the way your brand and products are presented on the Amazon marketplace, rather than waiting for a doomsday event or slow boil-over situation to command your attention.

---

[3] Certain materials in this chapter are reworked from the book authors' January 25, 2016 *Web Retailer* article titled "Vendor Central or Seller Central? 1P vs. 3P Amazon Strategies". This article can be found at http://www.webretailer.com/lean-commerce/vendor-central-or-seller-central. Reprinted with permission of *Web Retailer*.

We evaluate several common transition approaches that can be used to take back and secure more control of your brand—whether you're seeking to be proactive and prevent problems, or whether you're already experiencing one of the brand management challenges that are typical to Amazon.

We also review the important steps behind key tactics that brands can take to make these transitions easier.

We introduce tools and techniques that brand executives should consider using to help implement and secure new models of distribution.

We also look at several educational case studies in which brands shifted their distribution approach on Amazon, for better and for worse. We examine the specifics leading up to the changes, the mechanics of making the shift, and the results.

Chapter 5

We dedicate an entire chapter to the topic of product diversion, one of the core concerns most brands have about Amazon. While no single approach to limiting or removing grey-market sellers works consistently for all brands, there are strategies that the most successful brands use to manage this issue.

We explain why, if your products are being sold on Amazon without your permission or against your wishes, this is a symptom of issues elsewhere in your business—and what those are and how to address them.

We also cover how Amazon retail itself participates in grey-market channels, and meaningful ways to limit product diversion.

CHAPTER ONE

Amazon and the Five Pillars

At times, selling on Amazon can feel like watching a crazy Wild, Wild West shoot-'em-up movie. Sellers come and go all the time; you don't know who many of these sellers really are; they don't all play by the same rules or business logic you play by, their motivations may be quite different from yours, and there's usually someone acting irrational around the next corner.

Within minutes, practically anyone can set up a seller account and start offering a product that was sourced through any number of authorized, questionable, or completely illegitimate channels.

Amazon enables individuals and companies of all shapes and sizes to become sellers on Amazon. This is purposeful, as Amazon management believes that with more sellers comes more selection, and more selection brings more price competition and therefore more opportunities for Amazon customers. To Amazon, more sellers means customers can find the biggest selection at lower prices in stock, as compared with any other marketplace (online or offline).

We will begin by examining the importance of the Amazon channel to owners and executives of brands. We will first review the key objectives owners and senior executives typically have regarding their brands, and then we will examine the two business-critical questions about Amazon that any brand owner must be able to answer:

- What impacts can the Amazon marketplace have on a brand's business-critical objectives?
- What happens when a brand doesn't have an explicit, comprehensive Amazon strategy?

With the advantages that Amazon has created for itself on the marketplace, and the dominance of traffic it receives to its retail websites (averaging 188 million visitors per month, non-holiday), [4] ignorance is a risky option for the owners and executives of brands

---

1 Statista, September 2015.

who plan to leverage the Amazon marketplace for the foreseeable future.

Because the Amazon marketplace works differently from other channels into which a brand may choose to sell its products, it is important to understand what Amazon controls, and how it does and does not empower brands.

Successful building and maintenance of a branded business results from consistent and effective implementation of five concepts we term as Key Strategic Pillars. These pillars are:

I.   Branding
II.   Distribution
III. Pricing
IV.   Product Availability
V.   Catalog Selection

When any of these five pillars are ignored or overlooked, the underlying infrastructure of the brand can collapse fairly quickly. As you will soon see, the fact that practically anyone can become a reseller on Amazon potentially allows for decay to occur at a much greater speed than brands typically experience in traditional brick-and-mortar channels.

Let's evaluate each strategic pillar in the context of how Amazon works, and then examine the costs of ignoring or marginalizing the pillar.

I. Branding

To brand a product is to make and deliver on a set of promises to the customer about the product's physical, emotional, and service benefits. If done properly by the brand, the customer will learn and leverage these branding messages in anticipation of each upcoming experience when the customer buys and consumes this brand's products.

This "brand promise" is often packaged and communicated through media advertisements, in-store displays, point-of-purchase promotions, or sales team materials. In the online world a company website, an online ad, or a product detail page will likely be the primary source of branded material that allows a customer to learn more about the brand.

Let's say you represent Apple, and iPhone 7 phones are being sold on eBay. Due to eBay's listing procedures, every seller will create its own separate product page to merchandise its offer to eBay customers. Because of this listing process, customers must scroll through thousands of such listings (of the exact same item) to choose the retailer they prefer.

On the Amazon marketplace, Amazon has taken the approach of streamlining the catalog by having only one listing per SKU. Therefore, there would be only one listing for the iPhone 7, and all sellers of this item would be shown on the same page.

There is a lot to be gained from having a properly merchandised product page, as that content will be shared by all resellers of that product. The trick lies in ensuring that this page is, in fact, properly and professionally presented.

Typically, a first reseller with a particular SKU comes to Amazon and creates a "product detail page", containing important data such as product title, bullet points, product description, and SEO terms. That seller is said to have its own "offer" on this product detail page. For many resellers, this task of creating listings is a "necessary evil" that must be done before they start to sell the product.

By design, when subsequent sellers of the same SKU come to sell their version, all of the sellers' offers will be co-located on the same single product detail page. Multiple offers on the same page creates competition between sellers, as only one seller at a time can have their offer prioritized by Amazon as the "Buy Box winning offer" (which customers end up putting into their shopping carts the vast majority of the time).

While different resellers can provide content for the product detail page, usually the primary content on the page is contributed by the seller that first created the product offering and product detail page of that SKU, as described above. Then other sellers seeking to sell the same product simply add their offer to the existing Amazon listing (and leverage the existing product title, bullet points, product description, etc. that the first seller contributed).

If the content provided by the first seller wasn't particularly good (for example, if it's not SEO optimized, is missing bullet points, has a poor title or product description), that substandard content will continue to be the main content that represents the brand, even after multiple resellers add their offers to the listing. And all sellers of this SKU will be using the same poor content to market the product, unless one seller goes to great extremes to file support tickets with Amazon to get content upgraded.

Conversely, if high-quality content is initially used to create the listing, then all subsequent sellers will benefit from it. However, this can be a disincentive for the first seller to go to extremes to do something whose benefits can't be disproportionately enjoyed by the first seller.

Because Amazon product listing content scores well on Google, that product content – whether low, medium or high quality – will get indexed on Google, and may potentially show up higher on Google search results than the brand's content on its own website.

If product listings are created by some unknown grey-market seller, it's a pretty safe bet that the listing isn't going to get the same level of TLC that a branding or brand marketing manager would apply to the marketing materials they make available to brick-and-mortar channel partners.

And if your competition has figured out how to get high-quality listings created on Amazon while you haven't, your competitors' listings will have an advantage because they are more likely to be searchable/ discovered by Amazon customers. They're likely to have a higher customer conversion rate once customers see the product detail page content.

Besides the obvious risks and issues with substandard content created by grey-market sellers, 60% of customers want to see content that comes directly from the brands.[5]

The implication here for brands is that it is critical to make sure your product listings on Amazon are properly created and optimized in the first place.

There is a great deal of incentive to properly merchandize a product on Amazon by assigning someone to do the work of creating and maintaining optimal content.

Here are the key aspects of building an effective product listing:

Product Content

To maximize brand equity, a product's content should not only highlight product features but also explain to prospective customers its unique value proposition (UVP). Plainly said, an optimized listing should answer this question for the consumer: why should I buy this product instead of the competitor's?

At a bare minimum, Amazon customers expect standardized product content referencing the brand, product type, name, and any defining characteristics such as size and/or color. However, well-defined features and benefits and other well-written descriptive copy provide further strength to the brand's competitive edge.

---

[5] WP Engine Content Creation Study, May 2014.

It's unlikely that resellers meticulously crawl product catalogs and brand sites to write perfectly eloquent titles, bullet points, and product descriptions. That's why, as noted earlier, brands should contribute this information and lock it down with Brand Registry if they want customers to have an informed and enjoyable experience. Otherwise, when products arrive that don't match product descriptions, customers begin to distrust the brand and the brand's reputation is sullied. Or customers may forget or disregard a brand if its product listings lack enough descriptive content to even merit consideration.

Product Images

Amazon has strict rules about the look and feel of the main image for each product listing. These characteristics include a minimum pixel resolution, the need for a white background, and the absence of watermarks or wording.

Yet Amazon does not impose these same exact restrictions on secondary images, thereby opening up opportunities to showcase lifestyle images, and images containing clarifying text to point out key features. With nearly half of all Amazon shopping happening today through mobile devices, many customers rely more on product images than bullet points and product descriptions to educate themselves about the key features of a product.

If a product listing contains multiple high-quality images showing different angles of a product, lifestyle images of customers interacting with the product, and/or simple-to-read clarifying images, customers can easily differentiate a product from its competition—especially if competitive products don't feature additional descriptive images.

Product Reviews

As a customer, when faced with a product (or brand) you've never seen, how often do you look at the product reviews to assess its quality? On Amazon, the role of product reviews is often overlooked by new or inexperienced sellers, as well as by brand managers. Yet both a decent *quantity* of positive product reviews (at least 5 reviews) and a respectable average product review *score* (4 out of 5) can give credibility to your product and create confidence in consumers who don't have direct experience with your product or brand. It is important to recognize that the brand's sales are likely to suffer until this basic threshold of review quality and quantity is reached.

Through product review groups, or solution providers that help brands and resellers get more product reviews, it's possible to accelerate the process of building up initial product reviews on your product detail pages.

And since not all product reviewers are going to like your product, it's important to have someone keeping an eye on the average product review score and managing this area.

One approach is to manage negative product reviews, figuring out how to persuade those customers to remove or alter their feedback (within the scope of Amazon policies, of course).

If negative feedback can't be removed or altered, even a few low-score reviews can lower an average product review score enough to change prospective customers' perspectives. In this case, another way of increasing the average score is to solicit or cultivate more positive reviews to help increase the average score.

Unfortunately, we've seen many examples of brands and products being targeted by competitors who proactively leave undue negative reviews in attempts to damage the reputations of the brand, its products and its resellers.

We also periodically find product reviews with claims of counterfeit products. This is harmful not only because customers who see this review will question the product, but also because Amazon has automated systems that crawl the site looking for such claims. When

Amazon finds these claims, it usually suspends the listing and asks the seller to explain what's going on. A counterfeit claim can cost days to fix, requiring the seller to provide a lot of documentation to Amazon. And even if none of the counterfeit claims are legitimate, if a seller is involved in too many of them, that seller may be suspended or terminated from Amazon.

Promotional Positioning

Amazon offers a number of avenues for advertising products directly on the site. Some of these options are triggered by bidding on keywords that define a class of product. If a brand or product consistently owns those advertising slots, customers are more likely to see that brand or product as relevant. Consider, for example, an advertisement triggered by the key term "beauty cream." If a new or lesser-known brand bid aggressively on this term, it might win the advertising slot, so that customers see this brand and its products at the top of search results for this term. While that will also help *traffic* to these product listings, we also see advertising as a method for improving the perceived *quality* of a brand by creating awareness that it is relevant to key product terms.

BRAND REGISTRY: A KEY TO CONTENT CONTROL ON AMAZON

There is a solution that is critical to controlling your brand's content on Amazon. Amazon offers the Brand Registry program, through which brands can have their listing content locked down so that only one reseller can alter the content. Yet we estimate that at least 95% of all brands have never locked down their content in this manner.

A brand can create its own third-party account to become the seller solely responsible for the content. Some brands set up third-party accounts expressly for the purpose of creating clean listings for all their catalogs, and to provide authoritative content that can't be changed by other sellers. That way, when other sellers come along, there are *already* high-quality, optimized listings in the catalog, to which these other resellers' offers will be added.

Once a brand locks down content through the Brand Registry program, it can remain responsible for all content maintenance—or it can align with a single reseller to whom the brand can designate Brand Registry control. In exchange, that reseller must do the legwork to develop and lock down high-quality listings for the brand.

Even after quality product listings have been created, someone needs to watch the "hen house," given how many coy games other sellers can play creating duplicate listings that may not fairly or adequately represent your products and brand. We mention this because we have seen brands invest initially in building clean listings, then suspend ongoing oversight—after which new sellers create duplicate listings (using fake or new UPCs) to divert traffic to the new listings where only the new sellers are selling. Eventually, the brand's collection of listings can become polluted with these new, unnecessary listings.

Unless someone is looking for such listings, and filing tickets to get them removed or merged, the brand's overall representation on Amazon can be negatively affected very quickly.

Bottom line: we see the process of managing brand content on Amazon as both an initial investment *and* an ongoing process, ensuring that each brand is properly represented through its catalog's lifecycle. Regardless of how many units a brand is selling on Amazon (whether the brand is explicitly managing this channel or not), it is critical for the brand to secure its content so others can't change it.

What A Lack of Focus Does To Your Branding

Let's be clear: **whether you want your brand to be sold on Amazon or not, it will most likely end up being sold on Amazon by some reseller at some point.** All it takes is for little Johnny to get one unit of your product for his birthday, decide he doesn't want it, and resell it on the Amazon marketplace. Johnny lists the product on Amazon, where it becomes discoverable to millions of customers.

The amount of effort, accuracy, and completeness that Johnny puts into describing your product (and brand) will depend on several issues, but as you might imagine, little Johnny is not likely to do a stellar job of representing your brand. As we've seen, even well-established professional sellers often don't spend time building new product listings in a manner consistent with the product's branding.

And unfortunately, if a product listing has been created on Amazon through a sub-par effort, updating it to align with the brand's intentions isn't always easy.

Very quickly, your brand can show up on Amazon through several product listings that differ widely from one another in terms of quality and brand alignment. We regularly see products' brand names get replaced with the reseller's name, improperly classifying the product throughout Amazon's catalog. Or, a brand name might be slightly altered by a reseller trying to distinguish its own listing from an existing one that already has strong traffic or product review history.

Or a reseller will "squat" on a legitimate brand's UPCs, and use them for something completely different. Because Amazon's catalog is based on a unique UPC structure, once a UPC has entered Amazon's catalog (correctly or not), it's there forever—whether it was correct in the first place or not.

Even if you're fortunate enough to have properly created your brand's product listings in the first place, other sellers can subsequently alter the listing to their own benefit, in a way that may ultimately not be a fair representation of your brand. It's also entirely possible—and unfortunately quite common—for another reseller to come along and "hijack" the content of a fast-moving product listing, changing the product altogether to capitalize on the sales rank and product reviews of the original product.

Think about the SEO consequences of Amazon's catalog containing incorrect or incomplete information about your brand. Amazon is a huge advertiser on Google, so whether a customer is searching Amazon or Google for your brand, some seller's sloppy content could be the way that a vast number of online customers are introduced to your brand.

KEY QUESTIONS:

Because product quality isn't just about actual quality, but also *perceived* quality, the brand executive needs to address:

- Who is managing product quality perceptions? Do you have a brand steward looking out for your brand on Amazon? Who is going to do this work of creating and maintaining high-end content on your product listing pages?
- What investments are being made to update and continuously improve those perceptions?
- Who is investing advertising dollars in your brand to improve customer perceptions and traffic?
- When perceptions are hurt by negative reviews or claims of counterfeits, who is taking care of those issues quickly?

II. Distribution

The brand/company may not be the entity that actually sells the product to the end-user/customer. The brand/company might use a direct distribution model (wholesaling direct to the retailer) or an indirect, two-tier model (wholesaling to product reps or distributors, who in turn sell the product to the retailer).

With the advent of internet selling, it has been become easier for traditional B2B companies to enter the B2C channel by selling their branded products directly to consumers, whether through their own websites or a marketplace like Amazon.

Furthermore, a retailer's reputation can play into the customer's decision to buy the product. Even if a retailer has the branded product in stock, a customer may choose to shop elsewhere or buy a competitive product if there is some stigma or negative experience related to a particular retailer.

In a large channel with lots of customers, brands fight for visibility. In channels like grocery stores where there is only so much shelf space, not all brands will get the opportunity to present themselves to customers. But in an online channel like Amazon, there is no limited "shelf space"—*every* brand can conceivably be offered to customers.

That's why it's so important that brands do everything in their power to manage their visibility. Regardless of what distribution approach brands choose to use, brand owners should be asking themselves how they want to be presented to Amazon customers. Will they be presented poorly by a retailer who views the brand as just another set of widgets—or by a brand-dedicated retailer that invests in proper presentation?

Level of Competition

In brick-and-mortar channels, it is usually desirable to have your brand available in more places—whether that's more stores run by a large variety of retailers (most brands), or more stores run by a limited set of retailers (luxury brands). In brick-and-mortar channels, there is little to modest competition among retailers, as customers' search costs can be high (calling multiple stores, or traveling to multiple stores to check available inventory and prices). For example, while a customer might go into both Walmart and Target to look for the same product, the customer isn't likely to check in 20 separate brick-and-mortar stores.

On Amazon, the model is significantly different.

By Amazon design, every seller of the same product competes on the same product detail page. With only a small piece of real estate per product, each seller is competing directly with every other seller for the "Buy Box"—meaning that when a customer clicks the "Add to Cart" button, at any given time only one seller's offer can be put into the customer's shopping cart, and Amazon's "Buy Box algorithm" determines which seller's offer that will be.

While customers do have the option of picking the offer from any seller on a listing, we have seen greater than 90% of all non-media product sales going to the seller whose offer is in the Buy Box. It is critical focus on getting into that Buy Box winning position as often as possible. While the Buy Box algorithm allows for a rotation of the Buy Box winning seller, sellers can improve their chances of winning the Buy Box by having their offer in the Fulfillment by Amazon (FBA) program (where Amazon handles individual order fulfillment for the seller, rather than the seller doing the fulfillment itself), and by offering lower prices than every other seller. (See "Buy Box" in Definitions chapter for more details).

Brand owners should limit the number of resellers of the same product on the same Amazon product detail page, as too much competition breeds additional incentive for sellers to cut prices/break Minimum Advertised Price (MAP) policies, sell under a concealed business name, and/or divert product for quick sale to someone else—all behaviors against which brands should be protecting. When there is too much reseller competition, what is best for the brand is not what is best for the reseller.

21

To keep resellers motivated to follow the brand's policies, it is critical for a brand to control the distribution of its product on Amazon while giving them a realistic opportunity to win some meaningful share of the market available on each product.

We believe brands need reseller policies in place spelling out who can sell on Amazon, and indicating whether distributors or retailers are allowed to sell to other retailers. (Allowing resellers to sell to other resellers potentially creates grey-market sources of product).

If brands don't have such reseller policies in place (with meaningful repercussions for lack of compliance), then it usually doesn't take long for dozens of competitors selling the same fast-moving product to show up on Amazon. Many retailers look at Amazon as an easy place to sell a few more units quickly, even if it's at a lower margin. And for those sellers using Fulfillment by Amazon (FBA), it becomes even easier for resellers to conceal their true identities, as Amazon ships the order out to customers using Amazon logos, not the reseller's information. Placing orders on Amazon specifically to identify the sellers (a.k.a. "test buys") rarely reveals much about the true identity of the seller.

To summarize the downward spiral: when a brand doesn't keep track of what sellers are representing the brand's products on Amazon, product diversion and price undercutting kick in, and the brand gets degraded online. Next, the brick-and-mortar resellers start complaining that products are available at lower prices on Amazon, causing them to lose legitimate offline business to Amazon sales.

Many of these headaches and frustrations can be avoided if a brand creates a consistent pricing model with proper control of all distribution channels.

We share one particularly challenging situation where Amazon Retail approached a brand offering to wholesale it. The brand declined this offer, preferring to sell through its authorized online resellers. But the brand had a disgruntled distributor who sold huge

22

amounts of grey-market product directly to Amazon Retail. As a result, Amazon Retail still managed to sell the brand, even though the brand had declined Amazon Retail directly. Amazon Retail chose to sell the product below its own cost, setting off a price war (which Amazon Retail will usually win, since it doesn't have the same need to make money on each transaction, instead emphasizing long-term objectives like online distribution control of a brand).

These much lower costs on Amazon caused significant grief for the brand, as many of its brick-and-mortar resellers were understandably upset at the lack of pricing consistency. Some threatened to drop the brand altogether unless the "Amazon problem" got fixed. Fortunately, the brand had printed lot numbers on each individual product unit, and was able to locate and eventually close down the source of Amazon Retail's inventory. But because the brand didn't have 100% control of its distribution, Amazon Retail was able to access and sell inventory, setting off this distribution mess.

To make matters worse, Amazon Retail had an offer on the product and was able to control the listing content, overwriting the established Brand Registry. We have seen other situations where Amazon Retail incorrectly classified the product, resulting in a big drop in sales. In one case, it took more than a month to correct the Amazon Retail listing error as doing so required "approval" from the third-party Category Manager of the original category for the classification. Again, this only happened because Amazon Retail managed to source product outside of the brand's intentions.

In other situations, we've seen Amazon Retail approach brands that had poorly controlled distribution, offering to "fix" these problems on Amazon (i.e., by restricting which sellers can sell, or "gating" the product) if the brand agreed to wholesale only to Amazon Retail. As we will explain later, this exclusive sourcing relationship may fix one distribution problem for the brand, but may also create other problems down the road.

Going B2C, Overstock, Experimenting

Although we have talked about distribution challenges that the Amazon channel may represent to brands, itis important to acknowledge that it can also offer some big distribution advantages.

Firstly, with the use of FBA, a traditional B2B brand can legitimately develop a direct-to-consumer business as the third-party reseller of its own products. Furthermore, the brand can operate under a name different from its legal name (known as using a "DBA" or "doing-business-as" name) to sell online without revealing itself to its brick-and -mortar resellers. With such a third-party (3P) account, the brand can usually make higher margins selling stale or overstock inventory than it would if it were wholesaling this discounted inventory through its normal channels.

Finally, we really like how some brands have used their 3P accounts to experiment with different bundles and price points. Given how quickly a reseller can create or change listings, a brand can see if Amazon customers respond well to certain combinations of products, far faster and with much better data, than could be accomplished through brick and mortar resellers.

What A Lack of Focus Does To Your Distribution Model

For every brand we work with, we start with the assumption that using any distributors or sales reps runs the risk of the product being sold to someone that the brand doesn't want to be owned or represented by. Inevitably, when brands find their products being sold on Amazon by dozens (if not hundreds) of unfamiliar resellers, the cause is that at least one distributor has made a quick profit selling large quantities quietly to someone who isn't authorized to buy the brand.

Even with an explicit online reseller policy, the brand still needs to police its channel and make sure that the product is ending up only in the hands of the right resellers and retailers.

The brand also needs to make sure its distribution is tightly controlled worldwide, not just in the US. Otherwise, product intended for overseas markets can easily be reintroduced to the US Amazon marketplace through parallel importation or foreign grey market sales to resellers. As currencies fluctuate relative to the US dollar, the incentive to participate in such behaviors may become rather compelling, turning a normally honest distributor into one hungry for an extra sale to help make its quarterly numbers.

Some of our favorite turnaround stories involve brands introducing lot numbers, serial numbers or other mechanisms for tracking product through specific distributors, thereby allowing the brand to pinpoint quickly where the inappropriate sale by a specific distributor led to product unexpectedly showing up on Amazon.

It's critical for brands to understand that the ease with which resellers can "pile on" to a brand's product listings on Amazon, and how this adds to the necessity to determine which and how many resellers will represent the brand on Amazon. Otherwise, too many resellers add offers on the same product listing (meaning sales get split across more and more resellers), and new incentives surface for resellers to break MAP or divert product to other resellers through a quick sale.

KEY QUESTIONS:

- Does your brand know who is pricing and selling its products on Amazon?
- Does your brand have an effective online reseller policy in place?
- How big is the sales opportunity on Amazon for your brand, and how much competition is there across Amazon resellers of the brand?

III.   Pricing

Of all the strategic decisions the Brand Executive must make, pricing decisions are primary in determining how revenue flows *into* the brand company, whereas most other decisions impact how revenue flows *out* of the brand company.

While a brand's pricing strategy may have many layers to it, we boil the issues down to matters regarding how tightly pricing is managed during the product's regular sales life, and how pricing is managed when the product is at the end of its lifecycle. Not only is price level important to establishing how a brand is perceived by customers, but so is pricing consistency. If a brand is known to be regularly on sale, or cheaper in specific channels, it's no surprise that repeat customers will simply learn when and through which channels to capitalize on these lower prices.

It can be challenging for the typical customer to figure out the cheapest brick-and-mortar channel through which to obtain a brand. But the ease of searching online channels, along with the emergence of pricing applications that scour online prices, have made it easier for customers to find the lowest online prices—whether they plan to buy online or use that information to negotiate a lower in-store price.

Pricing Consistency

When a customer shopping different channels finds that the same product is sold at the same price across all channels, the brand has achieved pricing consistency. Price consistency pushes retailers to differentiate themselves on other characteristics—such as location, delivery convenience, availability, hours of operation, and so on.

While brands that own both their own brick-and-mortar stores and online channels (e.g., Victoria's Secret, Crate and Barrel, Starbucks) can achieve this desirable level of pricing consistency, most brands end up working through distributors or retailers they do not own or fully control. This invariably leads to some form of misalignment concerning incentives, where what is economically best for the brand is rarely what is economically best for the retailer or distributor. If pricing consistency is important to a brand, then that brand must work hard at policing its sales channels to make sure that consistent pricing is maintained.

If a brand is wholesaling product to Amazon Retail, itis important to recognize that Amazon Retail also monitors other channels for pricing inconsistencies — and that Amazon can actually demand that a brand subsidize Amazon for lost margin caused by such discrepancies.

How would Amazon lose margin on products when your channels have inconsistent pricing? To remain competitively priced for its customers, Amazon Retail will typically lower its prices to match another channel's prices on the same products. We know plenty of cases where Amazon Retail sent the brand a bill for the lost margin caused by this reduced pricing!

Price inconsistencies across channels not only send the wrong message to customers, but allow Amazon to capitalize on these inconsistencies.

Pricing Policies

A brand may implement a reseller policy such as Minimum Advertised Price (MAP), Manufacturer Suggested Retail Price (MSRP), or Minimum Resale Price (MRP). While legal stipulations and enforceability differ for each of these policies, each points to a brand's underlying desire to create consistent pricing across its multiple channels.

Whether these policies are unilaterally communicated by the brand, or explicitly agreed to by the distributor/sales rep/retailer, the brand will still need to conduct enforcement and spot-checks to account for at least periodic unauthorized price discounting within its sales channels.

Price enforcement in brick-and-mortar channels can be painfully difficult, as no brand has the resources to oversee the pricing of its products in every physical storefront across the country (or countries) every minute of every day.

It's not always easy online either.

While a multitude of existing software solutions can instantaneously measure and track price changes made online, pricing enforcement is often undermined by online retailers choosing to conceal their identities. Thanks to "Doing Business As" (DBA) names, a brand may not know how to find or reach an offending reseller/retailer even if it sees that prices aren't being respected.

As mentioned earlier, it's very easy for an Amazon reseller to conceal itself by using Amazon's FBA shipping services, in which Amazon-branded boxes sent to customers conceal telltale indicators of the reseller's true identity.

Overstock/Clearance Product

Maintaining channel-consistent pricing may not be as critical when a product is overstocked or at the end of its product lifecycle. But even then, a brand still wants to be the primary decision-maker regarding when its products can be discounted and by how much, rather than allowing retailers to make those decisions.

For brands that want tight controls over pricing across channels — including closeout / clearance items — it's important to understand the speed with which sellers on the Amazon channel can discount items, as well as the degree of discount they might implement.

With so many more customers shopping on Amazon than at any individual brick-and mortar-channel, it's often much easier for an online seller to clear through overstock/clearance inventory quickly at a slightly reduced price—a price higher than what a brick-and-mortar seller might use to move through the same levels of overstock or clearance inventory.

We see a lot of product sold on Amazon.com that was sourced through "retail arbitrage," in which the online reseller bought the clearance or heavily discounted product from one geographically-specific brick-and-mortar channel, and was able to resell the product at a high enough price online to garner margin from the transaction.

While capitalizing on these opportunities makes sense for retailers, the pricing discrepancies across channels again can harm the brand—and relationships with other channels. And the speed with which product can be sold online makes it very difficult for most brands to prevent such inconsistencies between online and offline channels.

What A Lack of Focus Does To Your Pricing

If you've worked hard to make sure you have consistent pricing across your brick-and-mortar channels, but not paid much attention to the Amazon channel, you'll likely soon hear about your failings from your brick-and-mortar retailers when they see your product available on Amazon at meaningfully lower prices.

And if customers learn to shop on Amazon ahead of any other channels—because there's a good chance some reseller will list the same item below your regular brick-and-mortar channel prices—it won't take long for meaningful numbers of brick-and-mortar customers to shift their purchases to online channels.

The Amazon channel is often the easiest place for a big pricing hole to develop. With online customers shopping 24/7/365, a brand must monitor its prices at all times (not just during the weekday hours of operation).

Fortunately, there are many inexpensive online price-monitoring services available. However, even once a brand knows who is selling at unacceptably low retail prices, it's hard to correct the problem unless it can determine the identity and contact information of the offending online resellers, or it can shut off their inventory supply.

While there are companies that specialize in uncovering resellers' real identities, these processes are nowhere near 100% effective. And they still leave the brand with the task of having to contact and/or file legal complaints or claims with these resellers.

Another potential challenge with pricing in the Amazon channel involves Amazon Retail. If a brand is wholesaling products to Amazon Retail, Amazon Retail may indicate it will respect MAP prices. However, Amazon Retail also gives itself an "out" to violate MAP if it finds others first violating MAP—and those violations needn't be on the Amazon marketplace.

Further, because Amazon Retail usually doesn't reveal to the brand in which channel it found the initial price violations, it can be next to impossible for the brand to correct the original source of price violations.

Finally, even if the initial offender disappears, Amazon Retail isn't going to flip back to MAP prices immediately if it believes Amazon customers have become accustomed to shopping at these lower prices.

KEY QUESTIONS:

- What is the brand doing to ensure its products are priced consistently across online and offline channels?
- When pricing inconsistencies occur, how does the brand handle complaints from retailers in one channel complaining about pricing in another channel?
- What's the overall cost to your brand for not having consistent pricing across channels?

IV. Product Availability

It's very simple: customers want immediate fulfillment. They want to find the products they want to buy. If they can't obtain products when they want them, they'll go looking for a different product.

Gone are the days of flipping through the Yellow Pages and calling multiple stores to find out which has inventory of a desired product. Today, a customer can go online and check Google, Amazon or a price comparison site, quickly establishing who has inventory available.

The greatest brand with the best features might be desired by millions of customers, but those customers will go looking for a competitor's product if that brand is repeatedly or consistently out of stock. The onus is on the brand owner to sustain product availability in the channels where large numbers of customers are searching.

If a brand sells its products to Amazon Retail, the brand must rely on Amazon Retail to replenish products in time to avoid stock-outs. If Amazon Retail changes its mind about continuing to carry a brand's products, rarely does the brand find out in time to secure another seller and ensure its products remain in stock on Amazon.

Alternatively, if the brand has only third-party sellers selling its products on Amazon (whether they are authorized or not), again the brand is reliant on those sellers to do a good job managing inventory forecasting and replenishment to keep the brand's products in stock. Since there is generally no coordination among third-party sellers or between Amazon Retail and third-party sellers, itis difficult for the brand to know with certainty that its products will always be available for search and purchase by Amazon customers.

When a brand's products aren't in stock, its competitors' similar and available products likely get disproportionate customer attention. A brand needs some sort of coordinated effort to ensure that all of its catalog is always in stock, while stale inventory is minimized and not inappropriately discounted within the Amazon marketplace.

<u>What A Lack of Focus Does To Your Product Availability</u>

If resellers don't do a good job of managing inventory levels, the product may be out of stock and hence unavailable to customers who will start looking at competitive or overstocked alternatives creating incentive for some resellers to reduce prices and clear through excess inventory.

Neither situation bodes well for a brand's desire to secure its positioning with customers and competitive products.

A lack of distribution control naturally leads to a lack of consistent product availability (or too much availability), resulting in undesirable pricing fluctuations.

KEY QUESTIONS

- How does a brand make sure that its products remain in stock all the time?
- If multiple resellers offer the brand's products on Amazon, how does the brand ensure there isn't too much inventory of certain products, thereby creating incentives for certain resellers to violate MAP policies or divert products elsewhere?

V. Catalog Selection

Based on our belief that a brand's products will end up being sold on Amazon regardless of whether the brand wants them there, the focus should be on ensuring each of the brand's products is represented in a manner consistent to its intentions.

If the brand has, for example, 100 different SKUs in its overall catalog, and today 80 are sold on Amazon by various resellers, what happens when someone decides to list one of the remaining 20 SKUs onto Amazon? Will the content used to build that new product listing be consistent with the brand's positioning efforts in all other channels?

With each reseller making its own decisions about what products to carry on Amazon, it is reasonable to expect that a popular brand's listings might be created by dozens of different resellers, reinforcing the likelihood that the brand is not consistently represented across its Amazon product listings.

And finally, with the possibility still in place that other sellers will create duplicate listings on Amazon (by abusing Amazon's requirements for each listing to have the correct manufacturer UPC applied to it), the brand will want to keep a periodic eye on whether duplicate listings have popped up, potentially creating customer confusion about differences across seemingly identical SKUs.

What A Lack of Focus Does To Your Catalog Selection

If a brand doesn't proactively address how each of its products is represented online, some reseller will likely invest less time and do a poor job (compared to what the brand wants) in building those product listings.

We encourage brands to at least create their own third party account on Amazon where the only purpose of that account is to lock down the product content of the brand's full catalog – that way, when another seller comes along with inventory to sell on that brand's products, a comprehensive and complete product listing will already be in place in the Amazon catalog for this new seller to use.

KEY QUESTIONS

- How does a brand make sure its catalog is available on Amazon, rather than just a random mix of products?
- Who is managing the process of ensuring new products are added quickly to the Amazon catalog, using complete and accurate listing information?

- Who is making sure the brand's catalog on Amazon remains clean of duplicate listings?

Summary

What creates a rich, consistent, satisfying experience for shoppers? This requires tightly controlled content, distribution, pricing, and well-maintained catalog selection and product inventory. If those areas are managed effectively, the Amazon marketplace becomes a sensible destination for your customers.

If you're not on Amazon, competitors will eat your lunch. Given Amazon's popularity and dominance, few brands are strong enough that customers won't replace them with another brand available on Amazon that meets similar needs.

Bottom Line: If you aren't proactively managing your brand in the Amazon channel, either directly or indirectly, your brick-and-mortar business will be negatively affected. Although the Amazon channel may represent only a small portion of your brand's overall sales, it is a critical channel to manage, for all the reasons outlined in this chapter, including:

1. the speed with which product can be sold online,
2. the ease with which prices can be changed online,
3. the ease with which customers can price-compare among online retailers, or between online retailers' brick-and-mortar channels, and
4. the ability of competition to directly impact your brand's representation and performance.

In the simplest of terms, **if your brand doesn't have an "Amazon strategy," you don't have an effective strategy for your brand overall** -- for pricing, for distribution, or for any of these other strategic pillars.

In the next chapter, we look at common options available for positively impacting your brand's ability to create and manage your Amazon strategy.

CHAPTER TWO
How Brands Sell on Amazon

Let us start with a tough reality for most consumer product brands: your products *will* almost certainly get offered for sale on the Amazon marketplace, whether you want your catalog to be there.

Few brands have complete control of distribution worldwide to ensure product doesn't get sold without its knowledge by distributors and retailers, or resold by consumers (as unwanted product or by retail arbitrage opportunists), including those brands that are comfortable with being sold on Amazon. They don't often have adequate control over how the brand is being represented or priced.

Even brands like Nike, who have sworn off ever being sold on Amazon, find that their products make their way into the Amazon marketplace through unauthorized resellers, grey-market sellers and product diverters.

And with Amazon's clearly stated policy that it is up to each brand to control its distribution (e.g., as long as the product is not counterfeit, Amazon isn't interested in removing product that has an unclear provenance), it's reasonable to expect those Amazon product listings will remain active as long as there is inventory available from any seller.

You may represent a brand that is prepared to fight to keep its products off the Amazon marketplace. If so, this chapter is not for you. Instead, we suggest you get the best distribution lawyers you can find, and work extremely hard to keep your channel tightly controlled.

But if you do that and *still* find that your product is showing up on Amazon, come back and read this chapter. We address the many options that a brand has for selling (or allowing sales of) product on the Amazon marketplace. We cover the costs/benefits of each option as well as how to leverage it.

Each option comes with its own set of issues, and must be clearly understood so as to develop the right "Amazon strategy" for your brand. These approaches include:

1. **The "Do Nothing" Approach**
Resellers sell without the Brand's guidance

2. **Selling to Amazon Retail (1P)**
Brand wholesales to Amazon through a Vendor Central/Express Account

3. **Multiple Authorized 3P**
Brand sells to multiple authorized third-party resellers

4. **Exclusive 3P**
Brand sells to an exclusive third-party reseller(s)

5. **Selling as the exclusive third-party seller of record (3P)**
Brand sells to consumers through a Seller Central account (B2C model)

6. **Blended 1P/3P approach (Blended)**
Brand wholesales to Amazon and sells to consumers via Seller Central

EXHIBIT A: The Six Major Distribution Models

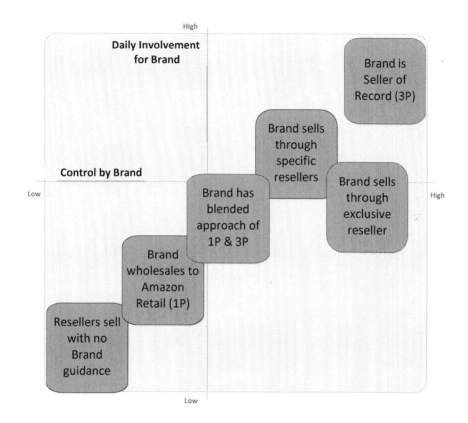

1. The "Do Nothing" Approach (No Brand Guidance)

Unfortunately, this is the most common approach for brands on the Amazon marketplace. Yet this "approach," or lack thereof, usually costs a brand dearly until it is replaced by something more proactive. Otherwise, someone else is going to manage the brand – someone who is not likely as motivated to do a good job as the brand's own team.

Sometimes it's a complaint from a brick-and-mortar retailer about sub-MAP pricing on Amazon that first alerts a senior executive at the brand to issues with the Amazon marketplace channel. This kind of wake-up call is often the first clue to the brand manager that this channel needs attention.

The brand discovers it is being sold by umpteen numbers of unrecognizable sellers on Amazon. The quality of product detail pages is highly variable, with low-quality content in the listings that frustrates customers who want useful information or have expectations about the brand. Pricing is likely all over the MAP too (no pun intended).

Good things rarely happen for the brand when there is no explicitly managed strategy for the Amazon channel. Pricing will be lower than desired, and sales will come from all sorts of unknown resellers; the brand won't have any insight into the total sales volume on Amazon, the brand content on the product detail pages will rarely be consistent with the brand's marketing efforts in authorized sales channels, and the selection and availability of the brand's catalog will most likely be poorly managed.

As a result, Amazon customers will receive an inconsistent and unbalanced presentation of the brand, leading to negative impressions and customer confusion about the expected brand promise. It can seriously damage a brand's reputation and competitive edge.

Whether a brand is small, medium or large, its presentation to Amazon customers will impact its growth rate on Amazon, and how it performs against other competitive brands. Often when a brand cleans up its branding act on Amazon, it will see a noticeable shift in customer preferences relative to the many Amazon-unmanaged brands.

As we detailed in the previous chapter, the longer a brand allows its products to be sold on Amazon with no central manager overseeing quality of product listings, product pricing, and catalog selection and availability, the more likely the brand is to run into trouble. It's almost guaranteed that duplicate or poorly presented listings will pop up, prices will vary widely from corporate standards, and availability will be unreliable. This disarray can become harder and harder to untangle.

Hard work and a lot of time can generally clean up a disordered situation with catalog, pricing, or distribution on Amazon. But as we've seen, resellers typically have little incentive to do this work for the brand. It's undeniably better not to get into this situation in the first place.

2. Selling to Amazon Retail

Amazon Retail, the "first-party" (or 1P) side of Amazon, is made up of Vendor Managers who seek to source items to sell on the Amazon marketplace. There are typically three ways that brands end up being sold by Amazon Retail:

a. Amazon Retail often looks at the brand's third-party sales, determines that the brand is selling well enough that Amazon Retail wants to start selling the brand itself. Amazon Retail then contacts the brand.

b. The brand creates an Amazon Vendor Express account, where it places its product pricing information into Amazon's ordering system, and the "Amazon computers" automatically decide if/when/how much product to order.

c. Amazon Retail purchases grey-market product from sources other than the brand. In situations where a brand has complete control of its distribution, choosing to wholesale product to Amazon may be a suitable solution for making quick inroads into the Amazon marketplace.

The brand can lock down high-quality listings and get sales going reasonably quickly via this channel. Dealing with only one retailer (in this case, Amazon Retail), the Amazon channel remains relatively easy to manage, with effort comparable to that of managing other large retailer customers. It's easier than dealing with multitudes of resellers.

For brands that are approached by Amazon Retail through option A above, it may be enticing to wholesale directly to Amazon. Brands may believe that this will mean not having to deal with third-party resellers.

Yet selling *to* Amazon, and keeping your third-party channel clean on Amazon, are *not* mutually exclusive. In fact, too many brands make the decision to sell to Amazon, yet don't do the work of keeping tabs on who *else* is selling their products—either on the Amazon marketplace, or to Amazon Retail via grey-market sources (per option C above). It's a common mistake.

What can end up happening is that Amazon Retail starts selling *alongside* other third-party sellers. And typically, Amazon Retail cuts its price to a level that ensures it wins the "Buy Box." (When a customer clicks on the "Add to Cart" button on a product detail page, the seller whose inventory gets placed in the customer's cart is called the "Buy Box winner." The winner is determined by a complicated algorithm that greatly favors Amazon Retail).

If Amazon Retail isn't already priced to win the Buy Box (for example, if another reseller is breaking MAP), Amazon Retail will break MAP to match the other seller's price, ensuring that Amazon Retail will still be the Buy Box winner. And if the other reseller then lowers its price again, Amazon Retail will likely follow (often in less than 15 minutes, thanks to computer-monitored pricing algorithms), resulting in a downward spiral on pricing—one that is very hard for the brand to control or reverse.

Adding insult to injury, we have seen many examples where Amazon Retail then sends the brand a bill for the original margin lost when Amazon Retail chose to match these lower-priced resellers.

So, when a brand doesn't have 100% control of its distribution, Amazon Retail puts itself into a position where it is always the Buy Box winner *and* gets paid its full expected margin. And the brand is left with a mess on its hands.

While the third option—Amazon Retail being a grey-market buyer of product—is not something most brands like to see, it is surprisingly becoming more common. Amazon Retail often uses a combination of these approaches: buying directly from the brand while supplementing product from "leaky" distributors. This gives Amazon Retail negotiating power with the brand; when Amazon Retail knows that it can source product outside of a direct relationship with the brand, it is able to push the brand on lower pricing.

When the brand doesn't even realize that Amazon Retail is sourcing product elsewhere, the brand also becomes ineffective in limiting or tracking quantities sold on Amazon.

In the next chapter, we review a number of factors that should be evaluated as a brand determines whether selling to Amazon Retail is the preferred mode of distribution for the brand.

3. Selling Through Multiple Authorized Third-Party Resellers

As brands become comfortable seeing their products sold on Amazon, it's common for them to designate specific brick-and-mortar sellers as the "authorized" resellers on Amazon, stipulating that no one else is allowed to sell product on Amazon.

This approach works well if each of the authorized resellers is willing to accept its fair share of the sales on Amazon, without trying to grow any further beyond that margin. This balance, however, can't be guaranteed. When there are multiple authorized resellers, inevitably each of these sellers wants to grow its overall revenue. This is a difficult feat to achieve without breaking MAP or making low-margin sales to grey-market sellers.

We have seen endless examples of brands that applied a MAP policy to a limited number of authorized Amazon resellers—and were surprised to discover that some of the authorized resellers sell below MAP during evening or weekend hours when the brand's team wasn't paying attention.

We have also seen authorized resellers operating a second Amazon account with a disguised name and breaking MAP prices to win the Buy Box, while the brand tries to unmask the disguised seller.

As this goes on, the authorized reseller either assures the brand that it is not the second seller, or the authorized reseller complains to the brand that these "unauthorized resellers" are hurting the authorized reseller's sales. Sad but true.

While a brand may have solid reasoning to reward good brick-and-mortar resellers with authorization to sell on the Amazon channel, it's critical that the brand understand how easy it can be for such online resellers to be tempted into—and get away with—such shenanigans on Amazon.

As we outline in the next form of distribution, we prefer to see brands limiting authorized resellers to one or two, with the stipulation that—in exchange for some distribution exclusivity—these resellers are expected to invest in the brand. This investment might be through optimization of product listing content, or through advertising expenditures to drive more traffic to the brand's product on Amazon.

4. Selling Through One Exclusive Third-Party Reseller

Rather than simply treating resellers as a channel through which the brand can sell product, a model using exclusive third-party resellers can help the brand better control exactly who is selling product on Amazon. If the brand has one (or two) exclusive reseller(s)[6], there is considerably more incentive for the reseller to work on getting better content onto product detail pages, invest in sponsored product advertising campaigns, and ensure that inventory remains in stock.

Under the model of a single listing per SKU on Amazon, it's understandable that most resellers don't take the time to invest in improvements that would get shared across dozens of other resellers. Moving to an exclusive distribution arrangement creates the right incentives for the reseller to invest in your brand.

It's also much easier for an exclusive retailer to do comprehensive inventory planning, since it doesn't have to account for inventory behaviors of other competing retailers. This helps to ensure that product remains consistently in stock (without too much excessive inventory).

We strongly encourage that such exclusive arrangements denote explicitly what the brand expects from the reseller beyond simply selling units.

With an exclusive distribution model, the brand can and should designate one reseller as the Brand Registry owner, responsible for loading and locking down product content optimized for SEO and customer conversion. This investment in creating better Amazon product detail page content should help the reseller to generate noticeably better sales volumes.

---

[6] The "two exclusive resellers" model can be meaningful if a brand has concerns that no single seller can ensure product always in stock, or if the brand decides to hedge its bets slightly to ensure that no reseller gains too much control over distribution on Amazon.

Typically, exclusivity is extended to a single reseller using a 12-month contract, with various approaches to renewing the exclusivity subject to performance on variables beyond sales revenue (such as those described above).

5. Selling as the Exclusive Third-Party Reseller

Sometimes the best long-term approach for a brand is to *become* the exclusive third-party reseller. Rather than rely on another reseller to do what needs to be done to represent the brand on Amazon, the brand enters the B2C space by becoming the only reseller. The brand then locks down content, works hard to keep other resellers off the listings, and enjoys MAP pricing and the retail margins that come with being the seller of record (rather than just the wholesaler).

For a brand with many brick-and-mortar retailers, it can be painful to prohibit them from selling on Amazon, but doing so sidesteps the challenge of favoring one such retailer over another.

If the brand doesn't price at lower levels than those it expects of its brick-and-mortar retailers, the complaints will die down quickly as brick-and-mortar sellers see that the brand is working hard on its behalf to extinguish price undercutting on Amazon—a problem that too often poisons the relationship between brands and their brick-and-mortar retailers today.

For brands that don't have individual customer order-fulfillment capabilities, Amazon fortunately offers its ever-popular Fulfillment by Amazon (FBA) program, through which sellers can ship items in bulk to Amazon's fulfillment centers across the US (and other countries where Amazon has international marketplaces).

The FBA program gives B2B brands a legitimate opportunity to manage the fulfillment of individual customer orders (B2C). In addition, products in FBA are also eligible for Amazon Prime and Amazon Super Saver Shipping -- two shipping settings that have been repeatedly shown to help sellers improve their customer conversion rates on Amazon.

Being the seller of record requires the brand to take on inventory risk, and potentially additional tax nexus liability (due to use of Amazon's Fulfillment by Amazon program). But profits offered by retail margins vs. wholesale margins often more than compensate for these issues.

While many brands don't have the in-house Amazon channel expertise or desire to set up a B2C division, there are companies that can help. For example, our company Buy Box Experts (buyboxexperts.com) is a service that provides end-to-end outsourced operations support, enabling brands to be the exclusive sellers of their products on Amazon, both in the US and abroad.

Accentuating The Managed Account Services 3P Approach

Some brands desire the "Selling as the Exclusive Third-Party Reseller" approach, but they either lack the expertise and resources, or simply do not want the responsibility of daily involvement of the direct to consumer business. So, they hire an outside agency to run the day-to-day Amazon operations. While the brand still owns the third-party account and the inventory, the responsibility of running the Amazon channel business is turned over to the outside managed account services business. This allows the brand to acquire highly skilled Amazon channel experts who deal with the operational aspects of being the Amazon seller of record, while the brand focuses its daily efforts on product development and sourcing. Revisiting Exhibit A earlier in this chapter, the brand can create a high level of brand control, while significantly reducing its daily involvement in operations and marketing.

The book's authors run a managed account services business for large brands, Buy Box Experts (www.buyboxexperts.com). As co-founders of PROSPER Show (prospershow.com), the continuing education conference for Amazon sellers, the authors also work with several other agencies similar to their own.

6. Blended 1P/3P Approach

For some brands, a suitable approach involves selling some SKUs to Amazon Retail, while selling other SKUs through a third-party account (whether the brand's own third-party account or some other configuration of third-party sellers).

Some brands like to offer their top-selling "hero" product through Amazon Retail, where the brand has access to additional paid merchandising and marketing opportunities through the Amazon Marketing Services (AMS) or Amazon Media Group (AMG) platforms. These opportunities can help the brand position its hero products against competitive products that are also big sellers on the Amazon marketplace.

Alternatively, some brands use this blended approach to ensure that any slow replenishment or stock-out issues by Amazon Retail are offset by alternative product supply available through a third-party account. As we have seen all too often, Amazon Retail doesn't always replenish in time to maintain constant availability. It may also decide to stop carrying certain SKUs, leaving the brand to fend for itself in terms of keeping products in stock on Amazon.

As long as the brand understands that Amazon Retail will almost always win the Buy Box when Amazon Retail has the SKU in stock (meaning the brand could have its own third-party seller inventory sit unsold for long periods), then the brand's third-party account can be an insurance policy for consistent product availability.

While no single distribution approach is going to be ideal for all brands, we have presented these options to help create awareness of the different models available. Ultimately, the right choice will come down to multiple factors that impact the brand's overall business. In the next chapter, we examine dozens of key issues brands should consider when selecting the optimal distribution approach for the Amazon marketplace.

CHAPTER THREE
Tradeoffs Across Amazon Models

Picking the right distribution strategy for your brand will require you to understand the pros and cons of each strategy, before choosing the tradeoffs you're able and willing to make. No strategy is perfect, and each distribution model has benefits as well as disadvantages.

As we've seen far too often, brands often make decisions about how they will distribute their products on the Amazon marketplace without properly understanding the full implications of their decision.

In this section, we review more than 20 business-related issues that should be considered when choosing an Amazon distribution strategy, and the potential impact of these issues on a brand.

We examine how each issue typically plays out relative to the pros and cons of each of the six distribution approaches outlined in the previous chapter[7]:

1. **Do Nothing**
2. **1P** (Selling to Amazon Retail)
3. **Multiple Authorized 3P** (Selling to multiple authorized third-party resellers)
4. **Exclusive 3P** (Selling through exclusive third-party reseller)
5. **3P** (Selling as the exclusive third-party seller of record)
6. **Blended 1P/3P** (Selling to Amazon Retail, as well as the third-party seller of record)

We analyze each issue requiring consideration in the same order of distribution approaches. To highlight which approach we believe is most ideal for the brand, we have highlighted that point with a (*) designation at the front of that preferred approach.

---

[7] Certain materials in this chapter are reworked from the book authors' January 25, 2016 *Web Retailer* article titled "Vendor Central or Seller Central? 1P vs. 3P Amazon Strategies". This article can be found at http://www.webretailer.com/lean-commerce/vendor-central-or-seller-central. Reprinted with permission of *Web Retailer*.

Given how many of these business elements and issues there are to consider, we have further organized them into three groupings:

A. Financial considerations
B. Internal operational considerations
C. Amazon-facing operational considerations

PART 1: Financial Considerations

CONTROL OVER PRICING

Amazon Retail states that it will honor a brand owner's Minimum Advertised Price (MAP) policies. Yet that is almost never true in practice, because Amazon Retail gives itself an "out" in that it can match any other seller's price (sellers on Amazon.com or other sales channels). It takes only one MAP violator anywhere for Amazon Retail to lower its prices and break MAP.

Once this price erosion starts, it's very hard to get Amazon Retail back to MAP. Since Amazon Retail's long view means it is prepared to lose money on individual transactions, the price erosion can go so far as to make the MAP price points meaningless.

As a third-party seller, the brand owner has 100% control over the prices it charges. Or, if the brand owner chooses to work closely with a trusted third-party seller, that control over pricing can also be tight, as long as the third-party seller honors the policy.

1) **Do Nothing:** Good luck controlling anything related to pricing. No distribution control means there is no pricing control. If MSRP or MAP policies are important to a brand, this approach to Amazon distribution is highly counterproductive.

2) **1P**: Amazon Retail may indicate that it will respect MAP/MSRP policies of a brand, but allows itself the opportunity to match

prices it finds elsewhere. Except for the large brands that Amazon Retail doesn't ever want to lose, this matching loophole basically equates to Amazon Retail having full control over pricing decisions for the brands it sells.

3) **Multiple Authorized 3P:** The more resellers of a product, the more those resellers must share the Buy Box opportunity, and thus compete head-to-head with one another to get the sale. This creates more incentive to lower prices or cheat MSRP/MAP policies. If there are 10 sellers all offering the same product at MSRP/MAP and all using FBA, it's likely each will get roughly 10% of sales as Amazon rotates these sellers' offers in and out of the Buy Box winning position. And if a seller quickly diverts products for a small margin to a grey-market seller, that seller might well end up making more profit selling larger volumes to a grey-market seller than it would by taking its fair share of the Buy Box.

4) **Exclusive 3P:** Any offer of exclusivity to a reseller should include clear stipulations and expectations about abiding by MSRP/MAP policies.

5) **3P(*):** The brand should have complete pricing control over its brand on the Amazon marketplace.

6) **Blended 1P/3P:** The brand should expect to have control over its 3P products' prices, while Amazon Retail may or may not abide by MSRP/MAP on the Amazon Retail listings.

COST OF SELLING

Amazon Retail will negotiate hard for low wholesale pricing, and will typically also ask for a payment of 4-10% to help cover so-called marketing or co-op costs. As sales increase, Amazon Retail may try to re-negotiate for even lower prices, or charge more fees for marketing or on-going account support.

On the other hand, when product is sold through the third-party channel, the commission fee to Amazon is fixed by category as a percentage of the selling price (typically between 8%-20%), and there are no additional selling fees to consider. If the third-party seller is using Amazon's FBA program, then there are other fulfillment costs, but those are competitive with any costs a seller might incur when fulfilling an order. All in all, we give the advantage to third-party, as costs are much more predictable.

While we recognize that a few brands have been given sweetheart pricing deals due to Amazon Retail's desire to source those key brands at practically any expense, it is more typical for Amazon Retail to pay somewhere between 50%-65% of the retail price as its wholesale price. Those prices do not include the extra selling fees such as co-op, freight allowance, damage allowance, charges for unreceived product, fees if purchase orders aren't replenished in time by the brand, and an extra fee for getting paid within 30 days (rather than the standard 45-60 days). By the time these fees are tallied up, there is typically more margin left over for the brand if it is operating through a third-party distribution model rather than a first-party distribution model.

1) **Do Nothing:** Even if you aren't engaged directly with Amazon, a brand may still incur costs when it finds itself having to recognize manufacturer warranties from unauthorized resellers.

2) **1P:** Those few brands able to sign sweetheart deals can make good money selling to Amazon Retail. However, the norm for most brands is that once they've factored in the additional and often unclear Amazon Retail charges, brands take home a varied amount of revenue after selling through a third-party account. However, if the brand sells only to other resellers/retailers, then

the Amazon Retail channel is likely to generate close to keystone pricing (50% off list price), comparable to wholesale pricing for many brands. As mentioned earlier, costs are not predictable when selling to Amazon Retail, as hidden charges can suddenly show up on invoices, resulting in payments to the brand that are much lower than expected. Many a brand CFO has complained to us that they never know how much to expect in payment from Amazon.

3) **Multiple Authorized 3P:** Your costs are comparable to those associated with standard wholesale distribution. It's not likely that a brand would incur any other direct or indirect expenses by selling product to authorized third-party resellers.

4) **Exclusive 3P:** It's hard to generalize here: some brands negotiate with exclusive resellers who are expected to take on some marketing expenses, while other brands are willing to contribute co-op money to a reseller that invests efficiently in promoting the brand on Amazon. Certainly, costs are much more predictable as there are fewer reseller relationships to manage, and the terms are usually very clear.

5) **3P(*):** The brand can predict what it will be paid relative to each dollar of third-party sales. However, it will have to cover the overhead and labor costs of managing the third-party account itself (or outsourcing those services to a managed account services firm, like the one this book's authors run).

6) **Blended 1P/3P:** The predictability and cost levels will depend on which products are sold through 1P and which are sold through 3P, consistent with what's described for those models above.

SALES VELOCITY

Amazon Retail has been known to tell brand owners that overall sales will grow substantially once Amazon Retail starts carrying the brand. Let's break this claim down into a few different scenarios.

If there are already third-party sales of the brand on Amazon, and Amazon Retail starts carrying the product, then yes, sales may grow overall. But the majority of sales will shift almost completely away from existing third-party sales to Amazon Retail sales, where the brand owner has far less control over the pricing.

In situations where existing third-party sales are already conducted through Amazon's Fulfillment by Amazon (FBA) program, dramatic growth is unlikely, as customer conversion doesn't increase much from FBA to Amazon Retail-fulfilled orders.

Sales will obviously grow from zero to something when Amazon Retail starts carrying a brand that isn't yet sold at all on Amazon. However, the issue remains regarding how much control the brand owner will retain over its brand.

Amazon Retail will also set annual sales targets for each of its brands. If those sales aren't happening, brands will be expected to spend on merchandising. Otherwise, the amount of attention that the Amazon vendor manager spends on the brand is likely to drop significantly.

There are too many other variables in play to comfortably say that any one approach is most likely to generate more total sales for the brand (while "Do Nothing" is almost certainly the worst approach).

1) **Do Nothing:** The brand has no meaningful control in this situation, as the brand isn't invested in the Amazon channel.

2) **1P:** Control of sales is shared. Amazon Retail ideally places purchase orders in time to replenish, and the brand fills those purchase orders in time to avoid stock-outs. In addition, the brand can set up Amazon Marketing Services (AMS) promotional campaigns to drive more traffic to their listings and improve customer conversion. But in our experience, promotional marketing dollars are typically more efficiently spent through third-party marketing tools if the objective is sales rather than brand awareness.

3) **Multiple Authorized 3P:** It's hard for the brand to ensure that at least one of its many resellers is always in stock on each SKU. Furthermore, it's unlikely that the authorized resellers will set up and execute Sponsored Product ad campaigns on Amazon, or do so adequately. Because these Sponsored Product campaigns work only when a reseller is the Buy Box winner, the brand's ad exposure will depend on if *every* potential Buy Box winner on a SKU has set up Sponsored Product campaigns at the same time to promote the same SKUs. Any one reseller may not see enough upside to invest in Sponsored Product advertising. That hurts the brand if its competition has constant Sponsored Product coverage.

4) **Exclusive 3P:** A seller that has an exclusive sourcing relationship with your brand will have a clear interest in seeing the brand grow. Because of that, coupled with the fact that the seller is the Buy Box winner, this seller is more likely to invest in consistently visible Sponsored Product ads. When negotiating exclusive sourcing relationships, we see some brands providing a specific monthly marketing co-op to the reseller, or requiring the reseller to invest a minimum amount each month for Sponsored Product ads.

5) **3P:** A brand that is the only seller of its products has full control over keeping products in stock, and promoting through Sponsored Product ad campaigns.

6) **Blended 1P/3P:** Depending on which SKUs are sold 1P vs. those sold 3P, the brand can promote its Amazon Retail listings through AMS, while promoting its 3P selection through Sponsored Product ad campaigns. There are Sponsored Product ads available through AMS too. However, those 1P ads will show up regardless of who the Buy Box winner is, so it's critical to make sure the brand has the products in stock. Ideally either Amazon Retail or the third-party branded account is the Buy Box winner (to capitalize on the ad spend).

PROFIT MARGIN

Selling to Amazon Retail will produce typical wholesale margins, as will selling to third-party sellers—but without any of the marketing or slotting fees that Amazon Retail charges. With Amazon retail, your wholesale margins will be squeezed over time, as Amazon Retail eventually pushes for lower prices or forces the brand's hand by sourcing the same products at a lower cost through indirect channels.

If the brand owner sells to third-party sellers, it will generate wholesale margins *without* the cost of fees that Amazon Retail typically charges brands for marketing and ongoing support. The brand owner may choose to sell as a third-party seller itself. That will produce retail margins, but there are obviously additional costs involved in running a B2C operation.

1) **Do Nothing:** No sales, so no margins

2) **1P:** As mentioned earlier in the Cost of Selling section, margins vary widely depending on whether or not a brand gets a sweetheart deal from Amazon. Most brands selling to Amazon make margins less than or equal to those of brands selling as third-party sellers—without the added cost of managing a third-party account. Margins made from selling Amazon Retail are also comparable to those made by selling to resellers.

3) **Multiple Authorized 3P:** Standard wholesale margins, usually.

4) **Exclusive 3P:** Depending on what the exclusive reseller and the brand have negotiated, margins should be in line with standard wholesale margins.

5) **3P(*):** Usually better gross margins selling as a third-party seller than selling to Amazon retail or to other resellers. Net margins should also be better, assuming that the brand is cost-efficient at running the third-party account.

6) **Blended 1P/3P:** A blend of margins, based on product mix in 1P vs. 3P.

GETTING PAID

While Amazon Retail typically offers 2% Net 30, Net 60, or Net 90 terms, third-party sellers are typically paid every 14 days (or seven days for a few larger sellers that have been blessed by the 3P category teams within Amazon).

Some Amazon Retail sellers have been asked to hire third-party companies to provide proof of delivery documents showing that inventory actually arrived before payment will be issued (even if the inventory balances in Vendor Central reflect inventory receipt by Amazon). Others have been told that they needed to pay Amazon

$25K in co-op (marketing) fees in order to receive about $250K in accounts receivable (refusing to simply deduct the co-op portion from the company's receivable balance). We have never heard of third-party sellers in good standing having problems getting paid.

When the seller gets paid on a timely basis, cash flow management is much easier, and investment in further growth is facilitated. When payment isn't made on time, the implications for a business can be staggering. We have seen first-hand situations in which highly leveraged companies have had to let go of staff and drop timely acquisition plans all because of unexpected payment delays.

1) **Do Nothing:** No sales, so no Amazon payments.

2) **1P:** It's usually rather difficult to get paid in full by Amazon without some luck and extra help ensuring that product has been received by Amazon. There are all sorts of hidden costs, and Amazon Retail has a habit of aggressively negotiating down prices as products get more popular on Amazon. It is not uncommon to hear about brands shipping thousands of dollars of product to Amazon, only to get paid 40-60% of what they expected, and explanations for the differences can be very hard to come by. Even if the brand believes that it is meeting all of Amazon Retail's operational metrics, mysterious return-related or defective inventory fees can be applied. It's useful for the brand's finance team to ask a lot of questions and get comfortable with unexpected variances when dealing with Amazon Retail.

3) **Multiple Authorized 3P:** Typically, the brand gets paid when the resellers buy product, just like any other wholesale/intermediary relationship. The brand knows what it will get paid, and as long as there aren't too many late or unpaid invoices, the brand can model its revenue streams accurately from authorized third-party resellers.

4) **Exclusive 3P:** The brand can predict revenue from selling to an exclusive third-party reseller in a similar manner to that described above for multiple third-party resellers. If marketing co-op or some other payment has been negotiated, that's usually a well-known, predictable cost for the brand.

5) **3P(*):** During the first few cycles of payment from Amazon, the brand will likely have a number of questions about how fees are charged by Amazon. The good news is that 99% of the time those fees are very predictable. A brand's 3P seller account using FBA may be charged for not preparing FBA shipments properly, but those situations are rare.

   Where we have seen problems is when a 3P seller account using FBA chooses to use its own carrier (rather than Amazon's UPS ground carrier arrangement) to ship items into FBA (if lost packages come to Amazon's fulfillment centers, it's up to the seller to file claims with the carrier, whereas FBA sellers using Amazon's UPS account are insured automatically). The other area of periodic concern related to cost variances involves miscounts of received FBA inventory (e.g., instead of receiving a case of 12 units, Amazon mysteriously receives 11). In most such situations, if the seller doesn't have a long history of under-shipping products, Amazon usually reconciles the shortfall if the seller asks.

6) **Blended 1P/3P:** Per above, there will be more uncertainty about being fully paid for inventory sold to Amazon Retail than with inventory sold by the brand's third-party seller account.

IMPACT OF PRICE DISCOUNTS

Running a short-term pricing discount on product wholesaled to Amazon Retail is going to cost you a lot more than featuring the same discount through a third-party seller account. Here's why.

Let's say you sell a product through Amazon Retail for $100. Assuming usual terms, it's reasonable to expect that you're selling the product to Amazon for $60, and you receive something like $52.80 after paying costs like the co-op fee, freight allowance, damage allowance, etc.

If you wanted to run a sale price of $75 for a short time on this $100 item, and Amazon Retail sold 1,000 units at this $75 sale price, Amazon would bill you $25 for each of the 1000 units, for a total of $25,000. Hence, your take-home of $52.80 would fall to $52.80 - $25.00 = $27.80 per unit.

On the other hand, let's say you sell the same item through a third-party account, again normally priced at $100. We'll assume you are paying Amazon a 15% commission, and a $7 FBA shipping fee, for a total of $22. So your net is $78.00. If you discounted the product to $75 for your sale period, your commission to Amazon is still 15% — but now it's 15% of $75 (or $11.25 instead of $15.00). Your $7.00 FBA shipping fee remains consistent. Now your net is $56.75 for product sold through a third-party seller account, rather than $27.80 for the same sale-priced product sold through Amazon Retail.

1) **Do Nothing:** No direct Amazon sales, no issues.

2) **1P**: The math above really tells the story about the impact of price discounting. We must also note that if a brand (either itself or through a reseller) discounts a product on another channel and Amazon Retail notices, Amazon Retail may match that discount — and then send the brand a bill for the lost margin caused by matching this lower price. Therefore, price discounting must be looked at strategically by a brand across all sales channels, since a selling relationship with Amazon Retail can become very costly if you're discounting outside of Amazon.

3) **Multiple Authorized 3P:** Unless a brand offers to subsidize a short-term price discount, the impact of the discount is usually

felt only by the reseller (and of course, Amazon receives a small total sales commission on the lower-priced item).

4) **Exclusive 3P**: Again, unless the brand has offered to pay for some of the price discounting, the reseller absorbs the full impact.

5) **3P(*)**: The brand as reseller absorbs the impact of the price discount. But, the net negative impact is usually a lot less than a similar discount offered through Amazon Retail discounting.

6) **Blended 1P/3P**: The effects will depend on whether the inventory is sold through Amazon Retail or a brand's own 3P seller account. And if the brand's 3P seller account has offers on the same SKUs sold through Amazon Retail, we highly recommend that the brand's 3P seller account *never* try to undercut Amazon Retail. It takes all of 10-15 minutes for Amazon Retail's pricing algorithm to match the 3P seller's price, most likely eliminating the 3P seller's short-term price advantage.

PART 2: Internal Operational Considerations

In this section, we evaluate factors which ultimately require the brand to modify how it sets itself up internally to put its products onto the Amazon channel. The mere act of selling on Amazon will introduce most of these issues, regardless of how the brand chooses to handle them.

CONTROL OVER BRANDING

How do you want your products displayed on Amazon?

What information is important to display?

Even brands with tight control over their distribution channels find that their product inevitably surfaces on Amazon. Therefore, it is important that the brand be properly represented so Amazon customers don't get the wrong impression. This means that proper images, product classification, titles, product descriptions, and other branding/marketing content and assets all need accurate, quality representation to ensure that customers aren't disappointed. In other words, the brand should have a "brand equity" plan for the Amazon marketplace.

Quite often, third-party sellers put the minimum amount of time into creating a product listing, resulting in the products appearing cheap or shoddy, with information that is confusing to customers.

As a wholesaler to Amazon Retail, a brand owner can list its products accurately and completely, and ensure that its products are represented in the manner they want. And if the brand is willing to pay Amazon Retail a substantial amount for superior product detail page merchandising (such pages are called A+ detail pages), the brand can get superior embedded images and videos on its pages. These features are not currently available through third-party listings (although we have seen some new sellers negotiate the ability to build A+ detail pages for a short-term period).

If working through one or two exclusive third-party sellers, or distributing as a third-party seller itself, the brand owner may have slightly higher levels of control over its brand (if it is proactive in submitting data) than it does when wholesaling to Amazon retail. That's because Amazon Retail can decide to alter branded content for its own purposes (something that can be avoided if the brand owner submits data through the third-party Brand Registry program).

1) **Do Nothing:** When a brand doesn't manage its catalog on Amazon, other resellers—known and unknown to the brand—will create product detail pages. The results are rarely complete

or aligned with the brand's standards for how to be represented.

2) **1P:** A brand can lock down its content in Vendor Central or Vendor Express, but making modifications to the initial catalog content is an onerous process that can be overruled by Amazon Retail. Yes—Amazon Retail can decide not to implement a brand's data if Amazon Retail believes it knows better.

3) **Multiple Authorized 3P:** Unless the authorized 3P reseller is given specific guidelines and content that it is expected to use to create the brand's listings, it is unlikely that any reseller will take the time to optimize listings the way a brand wants.

Ideally, one of the authorized 3P sellers would be granted "Brand Registry" permission—meaning the brand designates publicly to Amazon that it wants a particular 3P seller's content to be viewed as the authoritative content for the brand's listings. Content provided by a Brand Registry seller can still be trumped by Amazon if the same listings are also in Vendor Express or Vendor Central (whether they were put there by the brand or any other company that listed the items as available for Amazon Retail to buy).

4) **Exclusive 3P:** An exclusive 3P seller relationship combined with Brand Registry can be a good equation for motivating the exclusive 3P seller to step up and do the work of optimizing product listings. Ideally, a brand would negotiate this type of listing work as a precursor to or condition of the seller being granted an exclusive authorized (re)seller agreement. If the brand decides that more than one seller will share the exclusive relationship, then the brand still needs to decide which reseller will be designated the Brand Registry seller. The brand will expect more from that reseller to ensure brand content is properly loaded and updated.

5) **3P(*):** If the brand is going to be its own reseller, then it is essential that it be prepared to register for Brand Registry, and invest the work to lock down branded content on its product listings.

6) **Blended 1P/3P:** The tricky part here is that if a listing is in Vendor Central/Vendor Express and Seller Central, it can be changed through Vendor Central/Vendor Express only by filing tickets and trying to convince the Amazon vendor Support team that your recommended change is suitable. For some brands, Amazon lists in Vendor Central/Vendor Express only those items that they plan to sell through Amazon Retail. They list the balance of their catalog in Seller Central where they can still benefit from Brand Registry on those Seller Central listings.

TAX NEXUS

Selling to Amazon Retail is unlikely to create any new sales tax nexus for the brand, whereas selling as a third-party seller can create state tax nexus if the brand is storing inventory in Amazon's FBA fulfillment centers. On the other hand, if the brand has aligned itself with a third-party seller that does the actual selling, there is less likelihood that additional tax nexus positions will be created for the brand.

Recently, Amazon Retail has been highly vocal about tax issues with prospective brands, potentially creating a worry for brands that don't already have a multi-state presence. While additional tax nexus would require additional tax collection and remittance, a brand can retain external providers for those services that work with the Amazon marketplace. This issue is manageable if the will to sell through third-party is strong.

It's also important to understand that tax nexus can create income tax issues for the owners of the company. If a brand sells through an

66

FBA-activated third-party seller account, the resulting sales tax nexus could create an income tax liability for the owners of the brand in some of these FBA states. The tax can be based not only on the owners' investment in the brand, but also extend to the brand owners' other investments. Please consult with a tax attorney wise in the ways of sales tax nexus!

1) **Do Nothing:** If there are no sales by the brand, then there is no tax nexus to concern the brand.

2) **1P(*):** Amazon Retail is the seller of record, so tax nexus is Amazon's problem, unless the brand chooses to hold inventory in more states so as to be closer to the fulfillment centers where Amazon wants the brand to send product. Generally, a brand doesn't take on additional state tax nexus by selling to Amazon Retail.

3) **Multiple Authorized 3P:** If no sales to consumers by the brand, then no tax nexus issues.

4) **Exclusive 3P:** Same as Multiple Authorized 3P.

5) **3P:** If the brand fulfills orders itself (not using FBA), then the brand has tax nexus based on where it has its warehouses/3PL facilities (in addition to any other physical locations it has across the US, such as call centers, offices, etc.). The amount you are expected to collect will differ based on whether the states in question are origin-based or destination-based. For more details on this, please refer to an online tax remittance specialist, such as Taxjar, Avalara, Taxify or VertexSMB.

Also, a brand must keep in mind that, as long as its third-party account is part of the same LLC/corporate entity as other online businesses it owns, it is most likely triggering tax nexus *for all of those other parts of its non-Amazon business as a result of using FBA.* Please consult a tax attorney/online tax specialist for requirements specific to your unique situation.

6) **Blended 1P/3P:** Per above, while 1P doesn't affect tax nexus, activity in the 3P model will. And if any portion of that 3P involvement comes from the brand selling through FBA, then the tax nexus liabilities will be consistent with those incurred when the brand is the exclusive 3P seller.

MARKETING AND PROMOTIONAL OPPORTUNITIES

If you are willing to pay Amazon Retail for additional merchandising, there are more merchandising options available through Amazon Retail than through the third-party platform. Keep in mind, however, that unless your brand is considered one of the top ten to 15 strategic brands within a major category on Amazon (e.g., electronics, tools, and apparel), Amazon Retail is not going to pay much attention to you unless you spend heavily on merchandising. Instead, your brand's catalog will be treated like just another collection of widgets to be added to the already massive 300-million-listings+ catalog.

On the plus side for Amazon Retail suppliers, there are some marketing and promotional tools available with that model that are not readily available to third-party sellers. These include Brand/Store Page, A+ Detail Content, Vendor-Powered Coupons, Headline Ads, and the Amazon Vine program. However, this gap is closing, with recent initiatives made available by the 3P sales team on a test basis. While a third-party seller can create a pricing promotion, creating awareness of that pricing promotion is difficult, though Sponsored Product ads and Amazon Marketing Service programs can be used to drive awareness of third-party offers.

Interestingly, third-party sellers are more likely to be proactive and successful than first-party wholesalers to Amazon Retail in soliciting feedback from customers. And because recent feedback helps greatly with the search algorithm within Amazon (driven by a tool called "A9"), a third-party seller can distinguish itself with better search results on Amazon through proactive feedback requests. We know of examples where third-party sellers started selling wholesale to Amazon Retail, and saw their search results drop significantly relative to existing third-party competitors that were still able to solicit feedback.

Overall, the marketing and promotional opportunities certainly favor Amazon Retail, even if the wholesaler has to pay for these advantages.

1) **Do Nothing:** No Amazon presence means there are no Amazon marketing efforts to address.

2) **1P(*):** Amazon has created numerous ways for brands to spend money with Amazon on marketing initiatives (through Amazon Marketing Services). Some tools are more focused on building brand awareness, while others concentrate on driving direct sales numbers. While this creates more opportunities to market the brand, a common complaint we hear is that it's very hard to measure ROI on some of these tools, as Amazon doesn't share adequate data.

3) **Multiple Authorized 3P:** If a brand isn't selling product itself through 1P or 3P, there isn't much it can do directly to promote its product on Amazon.

4) **Exclusive 3P:** The brand may want to ask its exclusive reseller to take on the responsibility of running Sponsored Product ad campaigns. Because the brand will suffer in the reseller fails to set

up effective ads, we strongly recommend that a brand choosing to use an exclusive 3P seller retain some oversight of what sorts of advertising is being done on Amazon – and this may require the brand to kick in some marketing budget for the exclusive reseller.

5) **3P:** The brand can use Sponsored Product ads in Seller Central to do direct sales advertising aimed specifically at SKUs where the brand is the buy box winner, and they can also use feedback solicitation services to gather additional product reviews.

6) **Blended 1P/3P:** Again, this constitutes a blend of what's available through selling to Amazon Retail, and what's available to third-party sellers. The brand can leverage its Vendor Central/Vendor Express account to conduct advertising through Amazon Marketing Services (for both brand awareness and direct sales efforts), while also using Sponsored Product ads in Seller Central for direct sales advertising aimed specifically at SKUs where the brand is the Buy Box winner.

STAYING IN-STOCK

It's quite common for Amazon Retail to be unpredictable about keeping brands in stock. This means that brands selling through Amazon Retail run the risk of having no product coverage at any given time. Amazon Retail often seeks to obtain the full catalog from a brand initially, but will gradually slim down its inventory. Yet rarely will it notify the brand that it has chosen to stop carrying certain items. On the other hand, if the brand is selling through a third-party seller or *as* the third-party seller, it has complete control over when and what product is made available for sale on Amazon.

1) **Do Nothing:** The brand doesn't have any say regarding what stays in stock, as it isn't actively involved in controlling anything.

2) **1P:** While the brand can rely on Amazon Retail's forecasting models to predict when products need to be replenished (and place automated purchase orders to the brand), those models might be wrong, leaving the brand out of stock. Or Amazon Retail may simply decide not to stock specific SKUs anymore, removing those parts of the brand's catalog from consideration by Amazon customers. It's common for Amazon Retail to initially ask a brand to make all of its catalog available, but within months it changes course and no longer stocks slower-moving items.

3) **Multiple Authorized 3P:** Rarely can a brand coordinate across all of its resellers to make sure its catalog is fully stocked all the time. With multiple sellers each making their own inventory decisions, bestsellers can go out of stock, while other products may be overstocked. Overstocks can result in pressure for sellers to find ways to move the product, potentially outside the scope of a brand's MAP/MSRP pricing policy or anti-diversion policy.

4) **Exclusive 3P:** If negotiated properly, the brand requires the exclusive reseller to carry certain inventory levels, while providing a generous return policy to discourage reseller stockouts.

5) **3P(*):** With this model, it's the brand's job to perform effective inventory forecasting and management. Fortunately, as a reseller, the brand can fulfill orders in two different ways, creating a backup for out-of-stock situations in either scenario. As a reseller, a brand can offer product using Fulfillment by Amazon (FBA) shipping and via direct fulfillment by the brand company, so that even if FBA inventory is out of stock, the direct-ship offer is still available for the customer.

6) **Blended 1P/3P:** Some brands will sell to Amazon Retail, but also keep some non-FBA offers of the same SKUs in place as a backup

to ensure that the product is always in stock to Amazon customers. When Amazon Retail is in stock, it's unlikely that the brand's third-party offer would ever win the Buy Box and get the sale, so this is mainly a backup strategy. Nonetheless, we believe that part of the objective of a mixed 1P/3P approach should be for the brand to make its full active catalog available on Amazon, even if Amazon Retail typically gets the sales.

Some of these items might be slower-moving because the product listings are not particularly well set up, and Amazon Retail doesn't do any work to optimize the listing for the brand. We have had clients shift from 1P to 3P, and once we optimize their catalog, some of the SKUs that were slower-selling in 1P turn a corner and quickly become much bigger sellers.

DAY-TO-DAY INVOLVEMENT

If you are selling to Amazon Retail, you will likely need someone to check orders and periodically review product feed data to make sure it's current and accurate. Through Amazon's APIs (Application Program Interface: giving sellers access to Amazon's database) and Vendor Central portal, the process of keeping on top of inventory is reasonably straightforward.

If selling to third-party sellers, the process of wholesaling is no different than that in most other wholesale channels. But if selling as a third-party seller, you'll need to have someone dedicated to handling customer inquiries, individual order processing, inventory replenishment, pricing, product feeds, and so on. A good third-party seller partner will, of course, be able to handle all of those responsibilities within their current operations.

1) **Do Nothing:** Not applicable.

2) **1P(*):** Amazon typically orders product every three to seven days, so someone from the brand should be prepared to address open purchase orders fairly often. But rarely is the need instantaneous, and many brands simply assign the Amazon channel to an employee who already handles other channels or large clients.

3) **Multiple Authorized 3P:** Typically, there is no day-to-day involvement when selling to multiple third-party resellers, as those resellers are treated like most of the brand's other wholesalers/distributors/retailers.

4) **Exclusive 3P:** If a custom agreement is in place between the brand and the third-party reseller, some interactions may involve the brand, but day-to-day interactions are not common.

5) **3P:** Someone has to be managing the account every day of the year, as Amazon requires 3P sellers to respond to any customer inquiry within 24 hours. While some 3P sellers find ways around this (with out-of-office notifications for weekends), that can eventually catch up with the seller. We recommend playing by the rules and having a dedicated point person to respond to customer inquiries. Likewise, since Amazon's Seller Performance is always watching, it's important that someone from the 3P account be available to address any performance notifications that unexpectedly come in even on weekends or evenings. If the 3P business is at all substantial (at least 100 orders a week), it's likely that managing this 3P account will require at least 50% of someone's work week (including inventory management/ forecasting, listing optimization, catalog development, customer service, advertising campaign management, possible international expansion, etc.). It's a lot of work managing a 3P account, which is why many brands (traditionally B2B sales organizations) will outsource the day-to-day operations to

managed account services firms. Although it's a lot of work, it affords the brand the best control over its Amazon presence.

6) **Blended 1P/3P:** This constitutes all the responsibility of day-to-day operations for the 3P account combined with the work of replenishing Amazon Retail purchase orders. While these responsibilities typically fall to different people within a brand organization, the finance team is also kept busy having to keep track of two sets of books, as the 3P and 1P businesses are separate businesses with different accounting of inventory, costs/chargebacks, ROIs, and margin opportunities.

CUSTOMER SERVICE

If the brand owner sells to Amazon Retail, Amazon takes care of all customer service, including customer and competitor fraud issues. If the brand owner sells to other third-party sellers, customer service becomes the responsibility of the third-party seller, in which case adequate customer service can become a lot more variable. If the third-party seller uses FBA, Amazon will help with many customer service issues, but the third-party seller still has to deal with customers (or competitors posing as customers who may make false claims about receiving fake product). Given that most brands have a wide range of competitive brands on Amazon, it is generally more challenging to counter dishonest competitors if a brand owner is a third-party seller or uses third-party sellers.

1) **Do Nothing:** Not applicable.

2) **1P(*):** Amazon Retail handles all of this for the brand.

3) **Multiple Authorized 3P:** The third-party sellers are responsible for handling customer service and answering questions (typically on order status, refunds, and product specifications). If a reseller doesn't have a particularly good customer service group, the pre-

purchase customer questions may not be properly answered, leading to lower customer conversion or poor customer experiences. If the sellers use FBA, Amazon will handle most questions related to order status and refunds.

4) **Exclusive 3P:** This will work very similarly to the multiple-third-party seller model. However, the exclusive reseller and brand may work more closely together to develop a catalog of commonly asked questions that can be used by the reseller's own customer service team, or posted on product detail pages as "Questions and Answers" or "Frequently Asked Questions (FAQ)" for prospective customers to peruse. Amazon-supported customer service for order status and refunds is available on orders fulfilled through FBA.

5) **3P:** The brand should have the knowledge to answer customer questions, but may not have the bandwidth or desire to handle this. Ideally, whether there is an internal or external team handling customer service, that team would have access to the latest and greatest content to support customer inquiries. Amazon-supported customer service for order status and refunds is available on orders fulfilled through FBA.

6) **Blended 1P/3P:** Amazon Retail handles customer service on 1P selection, while the brand is responsible for customer service on its 3P selection.

BUILDING POST-SALE PRODUCT REVIEWS

Product reviews are critical to brand credibility on Amazon. Both quantity and quality of reviews are important. As a third-party seller, a brand owner can ask all of its Amazon customers to leave product reviews after the sale. The third-party seller can also solicit product review groups to buy discounted units, in an effort to create higher product review counts.

If the brand is instead wholesaling to Amazon Retail, on the other hand, the brand has no effective way of asking Amazon customers to leave reviews for products purchased on the site, because it is Amazon Retail—not the brand—that has the relationship with the customer.

Amazon does solicit product reviews, but their ability to acquire reviews is much lower than a 3P seller with automated review messaging services.

1) **Do Nothing:** Not applicable.

2) **1P:** No review options available to the brand. Amazon Retail can solicit customers' post-purchase product reviews.

3) **Multiple Authorized 3P:** The third-party sellers are in control of product review solicitation, and in our experience, they don't have incentive to spend the time setting up review solicitation software, or to spend money on that service.

4) **Exclusive 3P:** The exclusive reseller and brand may work more closely together to develop branding and messaging for communications with customers that encourage product reviews.

5) **3P(*):** The brand can utilize product feedback review software to solicit reviews from Amazon customers. The brand can also add its own branding to the message and control its content to ensure alignment with the brand's view of how it wants to be represented.

6) **Blended 1P/3P:** Review solicitation will only be possible for orders placed through 3P.

CANNIBALIZATION OF SALES FROM BRAND-OWNED DOMAINS

Brand owners that sell product through their own websites today often worry that selling on Amazon (either through Amazon Retail or third-party) will decrease sales via their own websites. While some sales decrease via brand website is typical, there is also usually a big increase in overall sales, because the brand is now exposed to more than 120+ million US customers (300+ million worldwide) who are already shopping for competitive products on Amazon.

1) **Do Nothing:** As we've established, your brand *will* get sold on Amazon whether you coordinate it or not, and when that happens there will be some cannibalization. But you aren't doing anything about it if you have no Amazon strategy! Cannibalization usually has the most negative impact when there are no controls by the brand, and unauthorized resellers offer the product well below MAP, making Amazon the preferred destination for value-based shoppers to buy the brand.

2) **1P(*):** If a brand sells to Amazon Retail, the brand will have exposure to huge numbers of customers, most of whom have never shopped on the brand's site. The brand now has a chance to be considered by many new customers, even in comparison to competitors. Rates of cannibalization from your own domain can vary from 5-30%; however, this is offset by the addition of new customers who otherwise might never have been exposed to your brand, or who might not have planned to shop at the brand domain website at any time soon.

It's important to note that if a brand sells to Amazon Retail, other resellers (including authorized resellers) of the brand aren't likely to get many sales on Amazon; their sales will be almost completely cannibalized by Amazon Retail, for the reasons outlined elsewhere in this chapter.

3) **Multiple Authorized 3P:** If there is price parity between the Amazon site and the brand's own domain, and the 3P offers are fulfilled through FBA, having the brand on Amazon should be a net win, even with small amounts of cannibalization.

4) **Exclusive 3P:** Same as Multiple Authorized 3P.

5) **3P:** The same is true for this model as with the above two third-party reseller models.

6) **Blended 1P/3P:** We often see brands making a small number of hero products available through 1P (to ensure high visibility), while making the remainder of their catalog available in the 3P account. In such situations, cannibalization rates are usually not very high, as long as Amazon Retail respects MAP prices used on the brand's own website.

PART 3: Amazon-Facing Operational Issues

In this section, we examine issues that may or may not apply for your brand, depending on what overall plans you have beyond the Amazon channel. How you handle these areas of business is not as likely to affect whether you see your products sold on the Amazon.com channel, but your internal Amazon policies in these areas can complicate how your brand grows beyond Amazon.com.

MULTI-CHANNEL FULFILLMENT

If you sell to Amazon Retail, you cannot use the same inventory to fulfill multi-channel orders, whereas if you sell through a third-party seller account using Fulfillment by Amazon (FBA), you have the option of using multi-channel fulfillment. This may not seem like a big deal, but many brand owners seeking to build a multi-channel sales strategy don't want to split inventory, or have to deal with individual order fulfillment capacity as overall business grows.

1) **Do Nothing:** Not applicable.

2) **1P:** Multi-channel fulfillment is not available for product sold through Amazon retail.

3) **Multiple Authorized 3P:** Any 3P seller using FBA has this option.

4) **Exclusive 3P:** Any 3P seller using FBA has this option.

5) **3P(*):** The brand's 3P seller account has this option if using FBA.

6) **Blended 1P/3P:** Multi-channel fulfillment is available on your 3P product selection.

FULFILLMENT CENTER PRODUCT STORAGE

The hundreds of thousands of Amazon 3P sellers using the FBA program have their products stored in Amazon's fulfillment centers. While the ease of using Amazon's fulfillment centers frees up seller time managing warehouses themselves and allows sellers to scale more easily, brands sold through some sort of third-party arrangement are subject to more restrictions than brands sold through Amazon Retail (e.g., space for hazmat or oversized products).

1) **Do Nothing:** Not applicable.

2) **1P(*):** It is better to have Amazon Retail manage your inventory for you, especially if it's oversized or hazardous. While other sellers may pay special storage rates at different times of year, 1P products are not subject to those changes since Amazon is responsible for making sure inventory is stored properly and won't melt. While Amazon does restrict storage of products vulnerable to melting in Q2 and Q3, for a special charge 1P sellers can have Amazon store and ship such products even during those quarters, so that this inventory remains Prime-eligible. Unfortunately, 3P sellers don't have this option.

3) **Multiple Authorized 3P:** For most 3P sellers that aren't selling oversized or hazmat products, there may be some concern with maximizing the fulfillment center inventory space that Amazon allocates. Realistically, Amazon will expand those limits if a seller consistently demonstrates the ability to sell through its FBA inventory at a fair rate. And if a seller doesn't move inventory fast enough, the impact of Amazon's unwillingness to provide more fulfillment center space will be quickly trumped by the steep storage fees that Amazon charges sellers for holding FBA inventory for periods of more than six months.

4) **Exclusive 3P:** Same as Multiple Authorized 3P

5) **3P:** Same as Multiple Authorized 3P.

6) **Blended 1P/3P:** If the brand seeks to have its products available for the Amazon Prime program, there will be incentive to have Amazon Retail carry hazmat products, Current storage space available to FBA sellers is highly limited, and realistically

restrictive to most sellers of hazmat products. To a lesser degree, oversized product space can be challenging to acquire through 3P, so brands may choose to sell such products through a 1P account, while pursuing a 3P distribution strategy for non-hazmat, non-oversized items.

SELLING INTO CANADA, MEXICO, AND EU MARKETS

If you sell to the Amazon.com Retail team, you are dealing only with the US marketplace, so your products will be sold only at Amazon.com. If you want to wholesale into Amazon.ca or Amazon.com.mx, you will require separate discussions with Amazon Vendor teams in each country.

You're much better situated if you are selling through a third-party account (whether with FBA or merchant-fulfilled orders). You can create a unified Canada/Mexico/US account and a unified EU account, and use these two third-party accounts to sell into these multiple marketplaces.

1) **Do Nothing:** Not applicable.

2) **1P:** Selling to these markets is not available without new vendor accounts for each individual marketplace.

3) **Multiple Authorized 3P:** Most 3P sellers can sell to these markets through conveniently consolidated accounts.

4) **Exclusive 3P**: Most 3P sellers can sell to these markets as noted above.

5) **3P(*):** The brand itself can create the unified accounts described above, to be the exclusive third-party reseller into these markets.

6) **Blended 1P/3P:** Sales to these markets will only be possible on product sold through the 3P account. A brand can choose to open up a separate Amazon retail vendor account for each of these other marketplaces, but each new market requires negotiation with a separate Amazon vendor team for each country.

SUPPORT FROM AMAZON

If you sell through Amazon Retail and you are not a big brand, good luck reaching anyone in Support unless you are paying at least $250k for dedicated service. As a third-party seller, you most likely won't get an "account manager," but at least Seller Support does respond and fix problems with your listings, inventory, payments, etc. There is no comparably responsive Vendor Central Support like this for Amazon Retail clients.

As a third-party seller, you have much more flexibility in terms of updating product images, titles, bullet points and descriptions, whereas a wholesale client must have all of its images and content approved by Amazon Retail. And Amazon Retail is often a lot more controlling or fickle in terms of what it allows, even if the desired changes are consistent with the brand's approach in every one of its other sales channels.

1) **Do Nothing:** Other than being able to file Amazon Infringement tickets related to copyright or trademark violations, a brand that does not actively participate on Amazon doesn't have many opportunities to interact to get content changes.

2) **1P:** A brand can file tickets in Vendor Central/Vendor Express to get listings updated, but the ticketing process is comparatively archaic compared to Seller Central ticketing support. You can get a vendor manager periodically on the phone or on email, especially leading up to big sales events like Prime Day, Black

Friday, etc. if you are willing to "pay to play" to get your products further promoted.

3) **Multiple Authorized 3P:** Multiple resellers may have contradictory views about how the brand's listings should look. And while each reseller can file tickets to get changes made, those changes can be overwritten by the next reseller's ticket. So while there is a clear path for getting support from Amazon related to catalog changes, the changes don't always stick.

4) **Exclusive 3P:** If the reseller has Brand Registry, then it's much easier to get content changed *and* locked down (so it can't be altered by others) by filing Seller Support tickets or by uploading flat file templates with updated catalog content.

5) **3P:** As with the exclusive reseller model, the brand can institute changes quickly through Seller Support or flat file submissions.

6) **Blended 1P/3P(*):** Items listed in Vendor Central/Vendor Express will get support from Vendor Support (Amazon Retail side), while third-party listings are supported by Seller Support. Interestingly, though, if you have a Vendor Express account with any SKUs listed, you can get some support on listings created only in Seller Central. We have seen companies successfully request A+ detail page content (videos, extended product descriptions) for listings that are only listed in Seller Central.

GETTING COUNTERFEITS REMOVED

While we just discussed levels of general support from Amazon, one area of critical importance to brands is what to do if counterfeits show up on Amazon. Unfortunately, the dynamics of the marketplace make it easy for sellers to introduce counterfeit products with varying levels of detection by other sellers, brands and customers. Nevertheless, as a brand, you want to know that you can get Amazon to address any detected issues of counterfeit products.

1) **Do Nothing:** If a brand's products sold on Amazon are littered with counterfeit product offerings and the brand isn't paying any attention the channel, the sales on the Amazon channel can quickly erode the brand's equity that it has built up elsewhere.

2) **1P (*):** We have repeatedly seen brands find that counterfeit offers disappear shortly after Amazon Retail starts carrying the brand. While there are various reasons why this happens, we have seen Amazon Retail be more willing to gate a brand (leaving only Amazon Retail's offer active on the site) if Seller Performance or Seller Support has had to deal with repeated customer complaints of counterfeits. We have also seen Amazon Retail proactively reach out to brands, and offer them more counterfeit protection if the brands move their products into a 1P arrangement.

3) **Multiple Authorized 3P:** Future customer conversion is at stake if a customer reads product reviews mentioned the presence of counterfeit products. It then becomes a community issue of addressing counterfeits on a listing – whether one or more authorized sellers, they all should be on the lookout for counterfeits, as they will likely all suffer if customers lose interest in the product due to such complaints.

4) **Exclusive 3P**: Same as Multiple Authorized 3P.

5) **3P:** It's usually easier for the brand to detect counterfeit offers when it is the active seller. But as with other distribution models, the brand must be diligent about tracking down the specific examples of counterfeits, and filing tickets to Seller Performance each and every time a counterfeit is detected – all in the effort to

remove both the counterfeit products and offending sellers from the marketplace.

6) **Blended 1P/3P:** For the brand selling to Amazon as well as through its own 3P account, getting counterfeits removed should be handled first through discussion with the 1P Vendor Manager. And if that doesn't work, the brand must remain aggressive in pursuing the removal of counterfeit offers by way of filing Amazon Infringement or Seller Performance tickets.

PROOF OF DELIVERY

Amazon Retail won't pay you unless you provide them with proof of delivery of your products to Amazon's fulfillment centers. And beware: even if your shipment is scanned as delivered to Amazon, that won't constitute "proof" for Amazon if it challenges your claim that the product was actually delivered.

Unfortunately, larger brands now need to hire outside agencies to obtain on-site, real-time confirmation from Amazon employees that 1P shipments have been delivered. If you are a third-party seller using your own shipping arrangements to get product to Amazon's fulfillment centers, you may face similar challenges with 1P customers. However, as a Fulfillment by Amazon seller, you are invited to use Amazon's partner carrier programs to ship your FBA products into Amazon's fulfillment centers. Most FBA sellers do use these partner programs, as they are typically much cheaper than anything sellers can negotiate for themselves, and the carriers provide Amazon with proof of delivery. This proof will be accepted by Amazon in cases where Amazon loses track of product after it has arrived at the fulfillment center.

1) **Do Nothing**: Not applicable.

2) **1P**: As stated above, proof of delivery for Amazon Retail shipments can be quite a pain. If a brand plans to ship amounts

larger than it can afford to write off, it's probably time to get an outside agency to ensure proof of delivery. Consider it an unfortunate cost of doing business. It's important to understand these kinds of inventory losses happen to all types of brands and products.

3) **Multiple Authorized 3P:** A brand's standard procedures for shipping product to any retailers/resellers will apply here. There's nothing unique about these sellers being resellers — unless resellers ask the brand to direct-ship product into the FBA program/channel. In this case, it is critical for the brand to understand issues related to carrier insurance (we suggest Amazon's UPS Ground account through Seller Central). Where the brand provides drop-shipping, the reseller usually sends the brand shipping labels (and possibly individual unit stickers) that the brand's operations team applies before sending the shipment(s) to Amazon's fulfillment centers.

4) **Exclusive 3P**: This model will work the same as it does when selling to multiple authorized third-party resellers.

5) **3P(*)**: It is imperative for the brand understand how FBA works. Once it has that figured out, then proof of delivery is usually automatically addressed by using Amazon's UPS Ground account. If the brand chooses to ship individual orders out to customers, the brand is responsible for providing tracking numbers on all orders — thereby providing Amazon, the customer, and the brand seller with the usual information about proof of shipment (and depending on the carrier, typically proof of delivery) to customers.

6) **Blended 1P/3P**: This approach will bring into play the considerations raised above regarding the Amazon Retail model *and* those relative to the third-party reseller model. Again, there is

much less chance of a proof-of-delivery issue occurring with third-party inventory than with first-party/Amazon Retail inventory.

SHIPPING LOGISTICS AND ACCOUNTING

As of mid-2016, Amazon Retail uses electronic data interchange technology (EDI) — an arguably antiquated system for receiving, acknowledging, and processing purchase orders. It also requires wholesalers to break up shipments among as many as a dozen fulfillment centers. Amazon Retail does perform inventory forecasting for suppliers, but only for 60 days in advance.

The third-party order replenishment system, on the other hand, allows the seller to palletize and ship to three or four fulfillment centers. The third-party seller does need to forecast inventory demand, and create replenishment orders regularly to stay stocked.

Amazon Retail commonly requires that you have your inbound shipments split into dozens of small quantities, routed to various Amazon fulfillment locations across the US. These routing decisions will impact whether you can realistically use parcel vs. LTL (less than truckload) shipments. Conversely, if you are using a third-party seller arrangement involving Amazon's Fulfillment by Amazon (FBA) program, products can typically be sent using LTL to just a few Amazon fulfillment centers, making shipping much more efficient.

1) **Do Nothing:** Not relevant.

2) **1P**: As noted above, shipping efficiency is generally not a strong suit of selling to Amazon Retail. Most larger brands suffer through the Amazon Retail process in exchange for whatever other benefits they consider worthwhile. As for the accounting data provided by Vendor Central, as we emphasize that it can be

an intensive task for a brand's finance team to keep track the less obvious and unexpected fees that can be charged to the brand.

3) **Multiple Authorized 3P:** In this model, shipping logistics and accounting aren't really an issue for brands, unless they are preparing FBA shipments inbound to Amazon fulfillment centers on behalf of their resellers.

4) **Exclusive 3P:** Same as Multiple Authorized 3P.

5) **3P(*):** If the brand is using FBA, it's quite common that the 3P seller account will be required to send an inbound FBA shipment to two to four fulfillment centers (and not necessarily the same ones as the previous time). But a brand's 3P seller gets to decide when it will create and ship an FBA shipment—whereas a brand through Amazon Retail is required to ship within specific timeframes of accepting Amazon Retail's purchase orders. (As discussed earlier, please also pay attention to any tax nexus implications of using FBA!) When it comes to accounting, the way 3P sales and payment data gets integrated into many accounting software packages could use some improvement. Xero Accounting has automated tools, while as of late 2016, QuickBooks is still not fully compatible with relevant Seller Central data.

6) **Blended 1P/3P:** This will be a blend of awkward and less awkward, depending on how much product goes to Amazon's fulfillment centers for Amazon Retail orders, and how much constitutes FBA shipments from the brand's 3P seller account.

ANALYTICS

Amazon Retail Analytics do cost extra, but they also offer valuable insights. Such analytic capabilities are not available to third-party sellers. (On the other hand, the Third-Party Seller Central portal produces much better accounting and general sales reports than the Vendor Central portal dedicated to Amazon Retail).

1) **Do Nothing:** Not applicable.

2) **1P:** The vast majority of 1P brands will use only the standard Vendor Central/Vendor Express data, which is not particularly insightful. The very small minority of 1P brands that invest in the fee for the Amazon Retail Analytics package (a cost of approximately 1% of sales revenue) is able to access a great deal of competitive intelligence data they can use to build their businesses. However, this enhanced data is not designed to streamline the general accounting for the business.

3) **Multiple Authorized 3P:** The brand doesn't see any analytics unless a reseller shares it. And each reseller can typically see only information specific to its own sales. This makes it difficult for a brand to get an Amazon-wide view of the brand's performance.

4) **Exclusive 3P:** Unless the exclusive reseller shares data with the brand, the brand will have no insight into its performance on Amazon.

5) **3P (* unless willing to pay 1% of 1P revenue):** If the brand is the only seller of its SKU on Amazon, then it can see a brand-wide performance view of detailed traffic, sales, conversion, revenue and listing quality through its Seller Central account.

6) **Blended 1P/3P:** The data accumulated from the brand that is the exclusive seller of its SKUs through its 3P account will provide much more insight than the 1P data, unless the brand has made the rare investment in the Amazon Retail Analytics package.

PAY-PER-CLICK (PPC)

When a product starts being sold on Amazon (whether through Amazon Retail or third-party sellers), Amazon will start bidding on pay-per-click keywords that it believes will drive customers to the Amazon site. If a brand owner spends money on PPC to sell product through its own website, once the brand is being sold on Amazon it may actually face new competition from Amazon for those keywords. However, since these same keywords are likely *already* being bid on by Amazon for competitive products that use the same keywords, we do not see this as a big deciding factor about whether or not to do business with Amazon. There are no real differences between distribution models on this issue, with a few rare exceptions in the case of 1P.

1) **Do Nothing:** Not applicable.

2) **1P**: When you sell to Amazon Retail, Amazon Retail will bid on keywords relevant to your brand. However, unless the brand is so unique that its keywords are distinct from all other listings on Amazon, it's likely that Amazon is already bidding on these keywords elsewhere. We don't see this as a big deal.

3) **Multiple Authorized 3P:** Amazon is most likely already bidding on your keywords, whether your brand is in Amazon's catalog or not.

4) **Exclusive 3P:** Same as above (for 3P or Multiple Authorized 3P).

5) **3P:** Same as above.

6) **Blended 1P/3P:** Not really a big issue either way.

HANDLING INVOICE DISPUTES WITH AMAZON

As a third-party seller, you have 12 months to submit a dispute and seek a refund. As a first-party seller (to Amazon Retail), you have only 30 days to pursue the same actions.

1) **Do Nothing**: Not Applicable.

2) **1P:** A 30-day window to pursue dispute actions isn't very long, especially if it takes a few weeks for the brand's finance team to figure out where the discrepancies are.

3) **Multiple Authorized 3P:** A brand isn't likely to get involved in disputes with Amazon using this model since the resellers will be responsible for dealing with any disputes.

4) **Exclusive 3P**: Same as Multiple Authorized 3P.

5) **3P(*):** The brand will have a full 12 months to contest invoice disputes. This is a generous window, though the brand should still have a clear process for keeping an eye on such discrepancies, and act on them expediently.

6) **Blended 1P/3P:** You have 30 days for your Amazon retail product, and 12 months for product sold through 3P accounts.

LIMITATIONS ON LISTING ATTRIBUTES

Amazon has restrictions relative to what kind of content can be loaded onto product detail pages by different types of sellers. We have seen first-hand how these differences can impact the customer conversion rates of the individual product detail pages by more than 25%.

1) **Do Nothing:** Not applicable.

2) **1P(*):** In what is known as "A+ detail pages," brands selling through Amazon Retail can create landing pages containing images and videos embedded in the product description text. Videos can also be separately loaded at the top of the page, next to the multiple images showing the product. These resources have not only consistently helped to improve customer conversion, but Amazon's A9 search algorithm also rewards such product detail pages with higher search results merely on account of the higher quality content contained on these pages. While A+ detail pages are not usually free to brands, the investment of time and money to getting these built often pays off with a strong return on investment.

3) **Multiple Authorized 3P:** We have seen several recent indications that A+ detail page functionality is becoming more available to third-party seller accounts, albeit for a fee. As this functionality becomes more available and affordable, we anticipate many more sellers leveraging its benefits to help customers gain strong understanding of the product offering through its additional forms of marketing media. It is also worth noting that Amazon rarely reviews images submitted by Amazon third-party accounts, so more deviation from the Amazon image rules can be seen on images loaded through Seller Central.

4) **Exclusive 3P:** Same as Multiple Authorized 3P.

5) **3P:** Same as Multiple Authorized 3P.

6) **Blended 1P/3P:** We like this approach a lot. A brand may get the high-quality listing content created through Vendor Central/Express, but use its Seller Central account to sell the

products, thereby getting the benefits of more pricing and inventory control, for example, through the third-party account.

SUMMARY

With so many issues to consider and tradeoffs involved with each Amazon strategy and approach, it is understandable that many brands end up working with Amazon Retail when Amazon Retail reaches out. On the face of it, the brand will have just one relationship to manage, and it is potentially a big, highly visible relationship. Sometimes Amazon Retail even promises some initial support with catalog cleanup or channel cleanup. And for a brand that doesn't have the time or skills to get the most out of the Amazon channel, working with Amazon Retail often looks like an attractive option.

In other cases, brands may not yet see the Amazon marketplace as strategically important because they have much bigger revenue channels. It makes sense to focus on your biggest channels, but unfortunately the Amazon marketplace often causes the bigger problems, so it needs attention too.

As we've established, the Amazon channel not only grows quickly, but is also the easiest for any seller to access; virtually anyone can begin selling product in this channel. With such a simple process for setting up a seller account, along with the FBA program, Amazon enables just about anyone with just about any product to sell —no physical storefronts needed, no sales licenses needed (and as we have seen too often, no proper attention to sales tax needed).

By allowing sellers to operate under "doing-business-as" names, Amazon has also made it easier than ever to sell product right under a brand's nose, while the brand is often not informed or able to control its Amazon position or address the inevitable issues.

When you find that your brand is being sold on Amazon against your wishes and without your permission, you are seeing the efficiency of an open market coming back to bite you. All potential failures in controlling distribution and pricing are magnified on Amazon, as it is a massive marketplace making your product available to huge numbers of price-comparing customers.

The Amazon marketplace can be a haven for grey-market sellers, so we believe every brand needs an explicit Amazon strategy to ensure control over brand content, distribution, pricing, catalog selection and inventory levels.

While the choice of distribution model for the Amazon marketplace is certainly a complex one, it has ramifications across a brand's entire distribution strategy, and should be made with full awareness of all the tradeoffs outlined in this chapter.

By offering an honest, objective assessment of the pros and cons of each key business element, we've hopefully empowered your brand to make a thoughtful and strategic choice. It should now be clear that, while Amazon Retail offers certain advantages, there are also many benefits to a brand leveraging the 3P channel—either through third-party resellers or by becoming the third-party reseller yourself.

CHAPTER FOUR

Transitioning to a New Model

In this chapter, we discuss how you can make better decisions regarding taking charge of your brand on the Amazon marketplace. We discuss how to proactively take charge, rather than waiting for a situation to boil over into chaos.

We evaluate a number of common approaches you can use when transitioning to an Amazon distribution model. We also review key tactics that brands can apply to make these transitions easier.

While no single distribution approach is going to be ideal for all brands (as illustrated in earlier chapters), it's important to discuss the steps required in the transition to each approach. Once a brand has made the decision to shift, understanding those steps becomes crucial.

The transition from one distribution model to another is often triggered by one of the following two scenarios, each illustrated by a case study:

1. **The brand already had some involvement in determining who sells its brand on Amazon, but the competitive landscape shifts quickly, causing alarm.**

   For example, an international apparel accessories brand with strict Minimum Advertised Price (MAP) policies sold its products on the Amazon marketplace through four resellers. This approach worked well for several years, and the four resellers took turns winning the Buy Box. The brand was happy to see that its products were typically always in stock through at least one of these sellers, and prices appeared to be stable. Although there were some MAP violations after hours and on weekends, the brand didn't take much action, seeing this as a small issue. Instead, the brand focused on developing its international distribution network.

   Within a five-month period, 15 more resellers showed up on the Amazon marketplace. The brand had no idea who these sellers were, and from where they were sourcing the product. Sub-MAP pricing became the norm, resulting in great frustration on the part of the original four resellers who were following MAP policies. With the competitive landscape in complete disarray, some of the original resellers exited the brand. The brand spent over 18 months figuring out who the new resellers were, and where they were sourcing what was clearly diverted product. In the meantime, the brand's equity fell considerably as the brand appeared to be always "on sale" from some new no-name seller with no sales history in this brand.

2. **Historically the brand has not been involved with who is selling it on Amazon, but a senior leader at the brand decides to tackle the "Amazon problem" because of the volume of complaints from non-Amazon resellers.**

For example: An international watch brand had no Amazon strategy. As a result, more than 100 resellers offered the brand for sale on Amazon without any resistance. While the brand had maintained Manufacturer Suggested Retail Price (MSRP) policies reasonably well in traditional brick-and-mortar channels, the prices on the Amazon marketplace varied wildly, in part because a significant number of grey-market sellers were willing to accept razor-thin margins.

Within a 12-month period, currency exchange rates fluctuated enough to make re-importation of product so attractive that another 150 resellers showed up with product, many offering prices well below wholesale costs for the same items in the US. Almost immediately, the level of complaints from U.S. brick-and-mortar business resellers escalated to a deafening level, forcing the brand to step in and finally proactively manage its brand on Amazon.

While these two scenarios differ in their trigger points, both demonstrate the interdependence of channels, in which control issues in one channel or country affect market dynamics elsewhere. Given the ease with which anyone can set up a reseller account on the Amazon marketplace, it doesn't take long for problems to surface on

Amazon in the form of more resellers, lower-than-expected prices, and diverted/re-imported product.

Generally, when such problems surface because brands have been undermanaging or not managing the Amazon channel, they are forced to actively step in and take control by implementing the most appropriate distribution model to remedy the issue(s) and prevent future problems. While in the last chapter we examined the pros and cons of each model from the standpoint of many different business elements, here we will examine the processes and considerations that come into play when shifting from one model to another — the chosen new model that will offer better control.

Tools and Techniques

Let's start by looking at tools and techniques that brand executives should consider to help implement and secure new models of distribution.

When some of our clients first come to us, they have as many as 150-200 unrecognizable sellers fighting it out for sales on Amazon. This is a desperate situation for a brand, and it can be overwhelming to figure out how to start the cleanup process.

The good news is that many brands *do* clean up this sort of situation — but only once senior leadership has made it a priority to invest in developing and rolling out an explicit Amazon marketplace strategy.

And once in place that strategy must be *maintained*, because the dynamics of the Amazon marketplace are such that all the hard work invested to clean up a channel can be very quickly undone if the brand personnel take their eyes off the channel, even briefly.

Three key techniques in this situation are:

A. **Online Reseller Policy / Anti-Diversion Policy**. The first task is usually rolling out a definitive online reseller policy that stipulates to all distributors, sales reps, and retailers that only specified companies will be allowed to sell the brand online (or at least on the Amazon channel).

Next, to the extent that the brand is able to identify the current resellers on Amazon, the brand can offer to buy back inventory in an effort to clean out the Amazon channel of any product it doesn't want sold. Unfortunately, because many resellers operate under a "Doing Business As" (DBA) name, it's challenging to root out the identity of many resellers.

Further complicating this issue is the fact that many grey-market sellers on Amazon are operating more than one seller account. This means they can quickly move product from one seller account to another, making for an extremely frustrating game of cat-and-mouse.

B. **Batch IDs**. The brand can also use serial numbering or batch IDs tied to specific distributors or sales reps. That way, the brand more effectively uses test buys of product on Amazon to figure out who is not playing by the brand's online reseller/anti-diversion policy.

We often find that the largest distributors and retailers are the most capable of cheating — either explicitly or through dishonest employees who have their own opportunities to work around company policies and divert product for a quick buck. Also, the largest distributors and retailers are often given the biggest volume discounts from the brand, giving intermediaries even more profit incentive for cheating (e.g., a quick cash sale of an extra pallet or two can easily put a few thousand dollars directly into a distributor's pocket). And, as the volumes sold to a particular distributor or retailer grow, hiding the redirection of a few pallets becomes much easier to do.

In one situation that we encountered, a brand discovered that at one of its largest retailers, a single warehouse employee was able to steal thousands of units of inventory without anyone noticing — because the retailer unconditionally accepted any shrinkage under two percent per month. Accumulated over thousands of units per month and many months, that two percent added up to substantial amounts of stolen inventory made available to product diverters.

In another situation, we saw wholesale club managers in the same city never putting product out on the floor to sell to their members, instead selling the product all in one sale (i.e., cross-docking product) to a grey-market seller. Due to a lack of in-store monitoring, the sale of such products would then simply show up on the wholesale club's accounting books as product that sold quickly in the club, thereby going undetected as having been grey-marketed in bulk.

In yet another case, a retailer opened additional store locations, then increased its order size far beyond what was needed for the new stores. With the reasonable explanation of additional demand due to new stores, it never occurred to the brand how much extra product the retailer diverted elsewhere.

Once a brand recognizes that it must conduct at least periodic channel policing, it becomes much easier to identify where inventory went, or where it came from.

Unfortunately, even if a brand manages to identify all of the current resellers on Amazon, it can take six to nine months for available inventory to be sold, bought back, or diverted to yet another channel, and finally free the Amazon channel of inventory from undesirable resellers.

Once the channel is clean of unwanted resellers' inventory, it's much easier to restore MAP pricing, if applicable. But until that point, sophisticated grey-market resellers on Amazon are likely to undercut MAP prices, resulting in pricing complaints from retailers in other channels.

C. **Branded content**. In parallel to the channel cleanup process, a brand can explore catalog cleanup. This includes populating product listing with brand-appropriate content as well as removing unnecessary duplicate listings of the same products within Amazon's catalog. (Such listings are usually caused by sloppy resellers, or resellers explicitly looking to divert customer traffic away from primary listings to newly-created duplicate listings of the same SKUs.)

As discussed in earlier chapters, the brand may choose to set up an Amazon third-party account of its own for the purpose of submitting and locking down branded content for existing listings (using the Amazon Brand Registry program), and filing tickets to have catalog issues fixed (e.g., duplicate listings, misbranded listings). When a brand does this, other resellers cannot easily alter listings or provide sub-optimal content. While a third-party account isn't necessary for a brand to engage in B2C sales on Amazon, it does allow the brand to address catalog inadequacies much more quickly and effectively, as opposed to relying on other resellers who likely aren't willing or able to make catalog changes.

Alternatively, a brand might turn to a specific reseller and grant that reseller the necessary permission to be the Brand Registry owner. With the appropriate paperwork from the brand, this reseller can submit and lock down catalog content that other resellers cannot modify.

With a clean channel and a clean catalog, a brand is well on its way to a solid foundation for building a high-quality business on Amazon through one of the distribution models we cover throughout this book. It's important to do this groundwork before choosing and transitioning to one of these models. Too many brands simply pick a new distribution approach without first getting control of the channel and catalog, resulting in ongoing messiness that causes their brand to under-perform long-term on Amazon. No matter how appropriate the new model might be for your brand, you won't get the most out of that approach without first doing the cleanup work.

COMMON DISTRIBUTION MODEL SHIFTS

Now, let's look at a few situations in which brands have shifted to a distribution approach on Amazon that better suited their businesses, goals and challenges. We will examine the specifics leading up to the change, and the mechanics of making the shift.

Shifting from 1P to 3P

We know an outdoor supply brand that had been doing several million dollars of wholesale business with Amazon each year. Initially enticed by Amazon's quarter-million-dollar purchase orders—at a time when the site was looking for sales anywhere it could get them—the brand signed a standard contract with Amazon to wholesale product.

Although Amazon had indicated it would respect the brand's Minimum Advertised Price (MAP) policy, within weeks Amazon used a poorly-understood contractual loophole to break MAP[8]. It had identified a seller on another channel selling slightly below MAP, and chose to match this lower price. Given the ease of price comparison that Amazon affords consumers, the brand's brick-and-mortar retailers were understandably distressed, and complained that they were being held to a different set of standards than Amazon.

---

[8] The loophole gives Amazon Retail the right to match another seller's lower price, regardless of whether that seller is a seller on Amazon or some other website. Unfortunately, Amazon Retail will rarely reveal the identity of this other seller, making it very difficult for the brand to address a pricing infraction with the seller.

With Amazon Retail no longer responding to the brand's constant inquiries about these pricing issues, the brand had to decide whether to fill subsequent purchase orders that Amazon Retail placed. Prices on purchase orders kept falling without any discussion, and the brand's accountants kept raising questions about significant unexplained deductions that Amazon granted itself on these orders. The resulting margin pressure, combined with the increasing brick-and-mortar complaints, meant the brand was forced to consider cutting itself loose from Amazon.

Dropping Amazon Retail as a client would have an immediate negative impact on top-line revenues. Recognizing this, the brand nevertheless calculated that short-term loss of sales was necessary to regain control of its pricing and margins across its channels, as well as to avoid losing any more disgruntled partners.

Once the Amazon Retail relationship was severed, the brand could regain its top-line sales and improve its bottom-line numbers by selling direct to consumers as a third-party seller on Amazon. Yes, Amazon's vendor managers threatened to enforce another poorly understood term of its standard contract with wholesalers[9] (Amazon

---

[9] Amazon's Product Availability Policy for Manufacturers states that "We welcome manufacturers to sell their products on the Amazon Marketplace. If you are a manufacturer and your products are sold by any other retailers or distributors, we expect you to offer Amazon Retail the option to source those products at competitive terms for sale as Retail items only." The policy goes on to state that manufacturers that only sell direct to consumers are exempted from this policy. (https://www.amazon.com/gp/help/customer/display.html?ref=hp_left_sib?ie=UTF 8&nodeId=201805990.) We have seen this policy challenged a number of ways by both Amazon Retail and the brand. When a brand is particularly sizeable, making it a "strategic" account for Amazon Retail, it may face some aggressive pushback when it tries to stop selling to Amazon Retail. Amazon Retail may threaten that the brand will be kicked off the platform, or that they will never be allowed back into 1P/Amazon Retail. Most of the time, we have seen the brands able to make the transition of moving part or all of their catalog over to third-party, while removing part or all of catalog availability from Amazon Retail. Some of the challenge with Amazon's Product Availability policy is that Amazon Retail will rarely agree to the same online reseller policy or MAP policy terms that the brand has in place with its other resellers – meaning, while a brand may shut off a retailer for breaking MAP, Amazon Retail rarely agrees to terms that give the brand that ability to turn off Amazon Retail for breaking

"expects" brands to give Amazon Retail the opportunity to buy products at the same wholesale price that the brand offers to other channels).

Within a few months, Amazon Retail stopped making threats and gave up on the brand. Top-line revenue has recovered, while bottom-line revenues are much healthier. Brick-and-mortar complaints have evaporated because the Amazon-generated MAP violation problems have disappeared.

We have seen this brand's story play out over and over with dozens of other brands that have been brave enough to make the shift away from an Amazon wholesale relationship. They have taken back control of their brands, their pricing, their inventory levels and overall coordination of all other distribution channels. The path is not an easy one to take, but it's often the only path that will enable a brand to manage its own destiny, online and offline.

Even some of the largest, most influential brands have made this journey from 1P to 3P.

There are key risk-reducing steps that we encourage brands to take if they plan to make this transition from 1P to 3P.

First, set up a third-party account, initially just to take control of brand content (using Amazon Brand Registry program) for any listings created by other third-party sellers. That third-party account ideally shouldn't have a name that clearly ties it to the brand (e.g., brand XYZ shouldn't name its third-party account something like "XYZ Sales" — this anonymity will allow the brand/third-party account to make changes without too much attention from Amazon Retail).

Next, in the third-party account, start carrying FBA inventory of top-selling items, essentially using that FBA inventory as backup

---

MAP. In addition, if the brand sees one retailer breaking MAP, it doesn't give permission to other retailers to follow and break MAP too. Yet Amazon Retail gives itself that right to do so through other terms in the standard Amazon Retail/brand contract.

inventory in case Amazon Retail runs out of stock (either by mistake or on purpose).

Then, begin the process of turning down Amazon Retail's purchase order requests, instead selling product in the third-party account exclusively.

Throughout this transition, if the brand has evidence that Amazon Retail is breaking MAP and/or buying supply of the brand from some other source (e.g., if some of the brand's SKUs that were never sold directly by the brand to Amazon Retail are now showing up as Amazon Retail listings), this may make it easier to challenge Amazon Retail on the one-sidedness of the current contract.

Shifting from 3P to 1P

We offer two very different examples of companies that moved from being exclusive 3P sellers on Amazon to working with Amazon Retail.

In one case, a health and personal-care brand was selling its top-selling product as a third-party seller on the Amazon marketplace. After many outreach calls from Amazon Retail's vendor manager team, the brand finally decided to start selling its products to Amazon Retail. The pricing terms looked good, and Amazon indicated that selling through Amazon Retail would lead to growth for the brand.

Within three months of sourcing product to Amazon Retail, the brand realized it had made a potentially big mistake. Sales were not improving, most likely because the brand had already been using FBA exclusively in its third-party account, so customer conversion rates changed very little in the shift to Amazon Retail-fulfilled. It became clear that the cost of leveraging any Amazon Retail marketing opportunities far surpassed the brand's budget. While Amazon Retail had asked for access to the brand's catalog, it became apparent that Amazon Retail had no intent of carrying the full catalog.

The brand needed to build a backup plan to ensure that its full catalog would be in stock on Amazon all the time (rather than relying on Amazon Retail to do so). The brand also needed to find a way to promote itself and its products without expensive marketing placement/slotting fees paid to Amazon Retail.

While the brand technically could provide product to other third-party sellers (especially on the SKUs that Amazon Retail wasn't carrying), few third-party sellers were interested, since any jump in sales on those SKUs would result in Amazon Retail purchasing those SKUs to start selling, precluding any third-party sellers from winning the Buy Box.

To fix this problem, the brand had to return to its third-party account and carry inventory on those listings where Amazon Retail was choosing not to stock product (the ability to do this is a potential advantage of a blended 1P/3P approach).

The brand also noticed that Amazon Retail was cutting the retail price of the products it *was* selling. While the brand knew that it didn't have 100% control of pricing in its brick-and-mortar channel, it was surprised to see that all of its products on Amazon were now being sold well below their expected online prices. This was because, as previously explained, Amazon Retail has the contractual right to match the prices of other non-online sellers' prices. Particularly frustrating for the brand in this regard was Amazon Retail's utter lack of willingness to show the brand *which* sellers' prices it was matching (which would have helped the brand address those pricing issues with those sellers).

And finally, since Amazon Retail had cut its prices to match other offline sellers, Amazon Retail then billed the brand for lost margin resulting from the lowered prices (a contractual right we also detailed in previous chapters).

The net result was that the brand ended up with a 1P relationship selling at retail prices *below* those it had commanded through its third-party account. Not only was the brand no longer taking home retail margins, but it wasn't even taking home wholesale margins, as it had to pay Amazon Retail for the lost margin caused by Amazon Retail's lowered retail prices. Overall sales on Amazon did not increase, and the brand still had to maintain its third-party account just to keep lower-demand products in stock.

Further, with products now sold through Amazon Retail, the brand was unable to increase its product review count anywhere near as effectively as it could have through its third-party account. Because Amazon Retail had effectively "cherry-picked" the brand's best-selling items, it was also no longer able to market the rest of its products through third-party marketing tools as cost-effectively as before.

In this scenario, the shift (which ended up not really being a full shift, but a 1P/3P blend) was not a good move for the brand.

In another 3P-to-1P scenario, a media brand with an extremely fast-selling product was approached by Amazon Retail to shift over to 1P. The brand resisted for nearly two years, as it was enjoying very high retail margins selling through FBA. Unfortunately, their star product was also one of the most counterfeited items on Amazon, causing daily frustration and expensive legal action to keep the Amazon channel clean. Eventually, addressing these counterfeit challenges came to constitute the majority of the brand's daily management activity for its Amazon business.

When Amazon Retail finally offered to lock all other sellers of new-condition product out of the listing in exchange for the brand wholesaling to Amazon Retail, the brand jumped on the opportunity[10]. Overnight, the product was no longer sold through FBA, and all

---

[10] While Amazon doesn't gate products very often, Amazon Retail recently introduced the Luxury Beauty category, and many beauty brands are now targeted by Amazon Retail offering to remove all unauthorized sellers in exchange for wholesale supply of product. (Remember this results in Amazon Retail being the Buy Box winner most of the time.) Unfortunately, such brands rarely have good control of their distribution and pricing *outside* of Amazon. As noted, Amazon Retail typically will price-match those non-Amazon sellers' prices, and this will result in lower overall margins for such brands once they pay Amazon Retail for *its* lost margin (resulting from Amazon Retail's price-matching reductions).

remaining FBA inventory was migrated into Amazon Retail inventory. The brand was happy to eliminate most counterfeit issues it had faced on Amazon, even though it lost a lot of margin by shifting from retail to wholesale margin.

Shifting from 1P to a blended 1P/3P

Here we profile two brands that made the move from 1P to a blended 1P/3P approach, for two very different reasons.

One brand had initially joined the Amazon marketplace when Amazon Retail approached it about wholesaling to Amazon Retail. After a couple of years of decent sales, but increasing headaches over never-ending pricing deductions and fees, the brand decided to go out on its own as a third-party FBA seller. The brand believed it would have much more control over daily marketing activities, and that it would be easier (and less costly) to introduce short-term price promotions.

The brand was very open with Amazon Retail about its intentions, and eventually decided to continue selling its primary "hero" product through Amazon Retail. The volume of individual orders was so large that the brand was happy to leave that fulfillment to Amazon Retail. Furthermore, Amazon Retail negotiated an attractive enough price for that product that the brand was better off than it would be selling it on its own.

Additionally, the brand targeted its marketing efforts at the parts of its catalog now being sold through its exclusive third-party account (using FBA). By doing so, they could accelerate sales faster (and more affordably) than was possible through Amazon Retail.

A key aspect of this brand's strategy is that, as this brand introduces *new* selection to its catalog, it is *not* making those items available to Amazon Retail. While Amazon Retail can technically require that a brand sell product to Amazon directly, via its product availability policy, we have found that Amazon Retail is much less likely to enforce its rights on this policy for new product selection that it has never carried before. Because of this, some brands have made the transition from 1P to 3P a success by consistently introducing new products only to their third-party accounts.

The second example is of a brand that also joined the Amazon marketplace after a call from an Amazon Retail vendor manager. After less than a year, the brand's CFO grew distressed at the unpredictable levels of payment from Amazon Retail for wholesale purchases. As previously noted, there were many additional fees without much explanation, taking up far too many hours of the CFO's time to track down. With so many other retail channels to handle, the CFO made it clear that something needed to change.

The brand started a quiet shift from 1P to 3P, where it became a reseller of its product. Using a third-party seller name that was in no way connected with the brand's own name, the brand began putting more and more selection into its third-party account, meanwhile refusing to fill the purchase orders that Amazon Retail was submitting. When asked why it was failing to replenish so many purchase orders, the brand replied that it was phasing out many products, and focusing more effort on its existing network of other third-party sellers that were already offering some SKUs on Amazon.

When Amazon Retail sent the brand a list of SKUs that it no longer wanted to sell due to low sales, the brand moved those items into its third-party account as well, put advertising campaigns behind those listings, and started to see a decent sales lifts for these items.

By stocking product in its own third-party account, the brand also faced fewer stock-outs of its better-selling SKUs—whereas Amazon Retail repeatedly ran out of product, and failed to submit purchase orders in time to ensure constant availability on Amazon.com.

Shifting from Uncontrolled to 1P

We mentioned earlier the recently-introduced Luxury Beauty program. We know of a brand that at one point had almost no control over who was selling its products on Amazon. The brand was very frustrated by the "leakiness" of its distribution network, with suppliers and retailers not abiding by the brand's online reseller policy. The brand entered the Luxury Beauty program, through which Amazon Retail agreed to remove all the unauthorized sellers. The brand did keep and authorize one reseller, while the brand itself continued selling Amazon Retail product to offer on Amazon.

Because of the Buy Box algorithm, which gives preference to Amazon Retail over third-party sellers, this one remaining third-party seller saw its sales drop off almost completely—despite having a price lower than or comparable to Amazon Retail's price. However, even with all unauthorized resellers gone, the presence of Amazon Retail did not improve things much. While the brand was initially able to restore its MAP prices on the Amazon marketplace by eradicating unauthorized sellers, within a few months Amazon Retail started matching lower prices that it had identified in other channels (i.e. Walmart.com, Newegg, and other major sites). Thus, the product was back to being sold at the lower prices that unauthorized resellers had set. And because the one authorized reseller was expected to continue to honor MAP, its sales dropped to basically zero (except when Amazon Retail was out of stock).

While the channel is now "cleaner," it's questionable whether the brand is any better off. Beforehand, it was selling product at wholesale margins, and even if the product ended up in the hands of grey-market sellers, the brand was paid wholesale margins by *someone*. With Amazon Retail as the big player on the Amazon channel, the brand cannot get wholesale margins because Amazon Retail charges the brand for the margin it loses when it matches lower prices found somewhere else. Meanwhile, the one authorized reseller who patiently followed the rules is deprived of sales by Amazon Retail.

This type of scenario is why, if a brand plans to move from uncontrolled to 1P, we recommend it evaluates whether it can address the lack of distribution control that initially resulted in so many unauthorized or grey-market sellers offering its brand on the Amazon marketplace. If the brand can't realistically control its distribution network, then it must decide whether it is prepared to pay Amazon Retail for lost margin when Amazon Retail inevitably lowers its retail prices to match lower off-Amazon prices. Amazon Retail *will* find — and charge the brand for — the margin it loses by matching lower prices offered by grey-market sellers.

Secondly, the brand should figure out how it plans to control its listing content. Once the brand starts supplying Amazon Retail, those product listings will be controlled in Vendor Central or Vendor Express, where it is much harder for the brand to make content changes, and Amazon Retail can overrule any changes suggested by the brand. (And yes, Amazon Retail apparently sometimes believes it knows how to describe the brand better than the brand's own marketing department.)

Finally, the brand will need to learn how to use the marketing tools available through Amazon Retail's platform (i.e., Amazon Marketing Services [AMS] and Amazon Marketing Group [AMG]) — both of which need to be initiated and managed by the brand's own personnel.

Shifting from Uncontrolled to 3P

Typically, in this situation, an executive with the brand realizes one day that the Amazon marketplace channel is so out of control that something should be done. The executive decides that "something" be the brand selling direct on the channel as a third-party seller.

So far in this book, we've illustrated many ways in which a brand acting as its own exclusive third-party seller on Amazon can be extremely beneficial. However, there are also challenges ahead when this model is adopted.

Chiefly:

    a. Most brands aren't experts in the ways of the Amazon marketplace.
    b. Most brands aren't experts in B2C selling, nor do they have the personnel to deal with B2C sales.
    c. Selling direct on Amazon doesn't automatically fix the distribution problems that caused the situation triggering this

move (in which multiple unauthorized or grey-market sellers were selling the brand's catalog on Amazon).

To successfully make the migration from uncontrolled to 3P, certain key changes need to be made by the brand. These include an aggressive effort to clean up its overall distribution, as well as the designation of a person(s) or outsourced team to run the Amazon channel.

In one case study from our experience, the presence of more than 150 unauthorized resellers on Amazon selling the products of a medium-sized brand triggered a response by the brand's executive team. After some initial analysis by a consultant, the brand discovered that many millions of dollars' worth of its product were being sold each year on Amazon.

For a channel this big, the brand needed a clear strategy and active involvement. Initially the brand launched its own third-party account, but wasn't getting many sales because it was overshadowed by lower-priced grey-market sellers. The brand also realized it had no clue what to do next within the rules and regulations of the Amazon marketplace. It then hired our agency to support its catalog and channel cleanup activity.

Initially, the brand cleaned up its product listings, putting up content that was consistent with its messaging in all other channels. Next, the brand locked down this content by using Amazon Brand Registry (as the brand owner, it was able to get Amazon to designate its third-party seller account as the account holding the authoritative listing content).

Channel cleanup was trickier, but fortunately this brand had batch IDs on its product, allowing the brand to identify which resellers were getting product from which distributors. While the brand had an online reseller policy, it had not effectively policed the terms of the agreement until this shift. The brand armed itself with guidance from a trademark attorney possessing online channel experience, as well as test buys connecting Amazon resellers to batch IDs on their products. In this way, the brand could safely terminate its relationship with multiple distributors that had been diverting products to unauthorized online resellers, or selling to other companies with online channels.

Furthermore, the brand made clear to all distributors that such diverting behavior would no longer be tolerated, and made sure that it communicated to its distributor network whenever it shut down distributors for this prohibited practice.

While the shutdown of wholesale supply to online resellers was an important first step, all the inventory that these resellers had in stock remained available for sale. It took a few months for these diverted inventories to get "sold through" on Amazon.

The brand also successfully filed dozens of infringement tickets with Amazon, showing how many of these other resellers were selling product that was materially different[3] from legitimate authorized product, thereby violating trademark law.[11]

Eventually, there was only one seller of the brand on Amazon: the brand's own third-party seller account. The brand swiftly secured MAP pricing again and locked down all of its content.

And for a while, things looked good.

Unfortunately, the story does not end there. One of the brand's former distributors, which had still not returned significant amounts of the brand's inventory, decided to unload that inventory to an aggressive grey-market seller. That seller in turn flooded the Amazon market with this newly available inventory. The brand's distribution cleanup and pricing recalibration efforts were pushed backward with

---

[11] "Material difference" is a tested legal concept indicating that a physical product may hold non-physical characteristics that make a grey-market product different from a non-grey-market product. These may be differences related to warranty, return policy, access to customer service/educational information, and quality controls (handling guidelines, storage guidelines). If a brand owner can demonstrate that a grey-market-sourced product has *material difference* from product sourced through channels that the brand authorizes, then there is precedent that Amazon will remove the grey-market seller's offer from the Amazon marketplace.

the presence of this grey-market seller who was selling well below MAP.

Shortly thereafter, *another* reseller popped up. This time it was Amazon Retail itself, which had also grey-market-sourced the brand after their multiple offers to wholesale it were declined. With Amazon Retail in possession of product, Amazon owned the listing content (while the brand didn't even have a Vendor Central account through which it could file tickets to get its listings updated).

Amazon Retail also owned the Buy Box on the product. It went so far as to have its vendor manager tell the brand that Amazon Retail would continue to sell the product via this grey-market source until the brand agreed to wholesale to Amazon Retail.

Clearly the brand's behind-the-scenes distribution cleanup work had not been properly completed, leaving this gaping hole on the Amazon marketplace.

While this saga may play out through many more chapters, the moral of this story is that it doesn't take much for a seemingly cleaned-up Amazon channel to get messy again—and Amazon Retail itself can very well be the culprit for some of the continued commotion.

Why Giving Up on Amazon Isn't the Answer

Finally, below we include two examples of other commonplace scenarios involving Amazon Retail. It is worth including such cautionary tales so that brands can see what can happen if they simply throw up their arms and give up on the Amazon channel.

Shifting from 1P to Uncontrolled 3P

A large outdoor apparel brand had been selling its full catalog to Amazon Retail for many years. As the years went on, the brand became increasingly frustrated with the hidden fees and aggressive negotiations by Amazon Retail to continually lower wholesale prices. The brand believed that it should be getting much more consistent commitment and cooperation, given its long-term partnership with

Amazon Retail. Even with an assigned team consisting of a vendor manager and support reps that the brand could call any time, the brand still felt thwarted by its dealings with Amazon.

While there were a few unidentified and unauthorized third-party sellers on the Amazon marketplace, the brand didn't focus (or need to focus) on them, as Amazon Retail was typically winning the Buy Box on most product listings.

Eventually the brand decided to stop selling to Amazon Retail. Publicly, it told Amazon Retail that it was no longer willing to do business, and instead the brand let the collection of uncontrolled third-party sellers win the Buy Box (once Amazon Retail ran out of stock).

With Amazon Retail out of the mix, it didn't take long for sales to pick up for individual resellers, thereby creating incentive for additional unidentified or unauthorized resellers to find product and start offering it on Amazon. The landscape for this brand's product on Amazon thus became a complete free-for-all. New catalog offerings were created with little effort by whatever unauthorized seller got hold of product first. Adherence to MAP pricing policies became non-existent. Key SKUs were regularly out of stock, because there was no central oversight to make sure these SKUs remained in stock. And lack of MAP pricing created more discontent among the brand's brick-and-mortar retailers, who were not allowed to offer the same low price points as resellers on Amazon.

Should this brand ever decide to become active again in this channel, the amount of cleanup work ahead is daunting.

Managing 1P/Uncontrolled 3P

There are some important nuances to note regarding how different types of Amazon accounts can be used to address issues beyond distribution or pricing.

A Fortune 500 company with an extensive collection of consumer brands was selling 1P to Amazon Retail, while at the same time dealing with hundreds of unidentified third-party sellers also offering its product on the Amazon marketplace. Literally dozens of duplicate listings were starting to show up in the Amazon catalog. This resulted not only in customer traffic being diverted to secondary listings, but the brand losing a clear view of how much of each of its brands was being sold on the Amazon marketplace.

While the company didn't plan to change how it did business with Amazon Retail, it opened a third-party account specifically to clean up all the 3P listings that were duplicates of the Amazon Retail listings. By doing so, it was able to secure Brand Registry and lock down quality branded content; add offers for non-1P listings to its third-party account, and identify duplicate (usually higher-priced) listings.

By merging several thousand duplicate listings into the (usually lower-priced) Amazon Retail listings, this company cleaned up its overall Amazon presence. With multiple listings for each SKU combined onto a single product listing (represented by a single Amazon Stock Inventory Number, or ASIN), it became much easier for the company to keep its branded content consistent and high-quality across all Amazon listings — not just the Amazon Retail ones.

The company took control of listings that were not in Amazon Retail's catalog by creating an offer on that listing in its third-party account.

The company didn't sell anything itself through its third-party account, instead merely using the third-party account as a mechanism for cleaning up and controlling the content of all listings not in the Amazon Retail catalog (i.e., third-party listings by other resellers).

This catalog cleanup work enabled the company to regain a clear view of exact sales quantity for each of its brands and products across the Amazon marketplace, allowing it to invest more strategically in promotions based on how brands or products were selling.

In addition, its marketing efforts through Amazon Retail became much more efficient: with the duplicate listings gone, all Amazon customer traffic for a particular SKU was directed to only one listing, making advertising for that SKU much more likely to convert.

Conclusion

The common theme across these examples is that clear paths do exist by which executives can take control of their brands on the Amazon marketplace. Some paths involve more complex efforts than others to untangle and heal messes created by a prior lack of attention to the Amazon channel (or by a prior decision to sell directly to Amazon Retail). Sometimes a model shift works beautifully and ideally; and other times it is a mixed experience that is still preferable to the previous scenario.

Regardless, it is critical for the leadership team of any brand to develop and implement a proactive presence on the Amazon marketplace, rather than letting others make potentially dangerous decisions that will hamper the brand's positions beyond Amazon.

CHAPTER FIVE
Untangling the Product Diversion Mess

"Why is my brand being sold on Amazon?"

"Who are these sellers?"

"How did they get my products?"

"How do I get rid of these sellers?"

While Amazon is an open marketplace where practically anyone with product can sell it, **the marketplace isn't the *cause* of your product being sold there**. Your products being sold on Amazon without your permission or against your wishes, this is a symptom of issues elsewhere in your business. Those issues create conditions that allow your products to be made available on Amazon without your express participation or control.

Here's a typical scenario for start-up brands:

Your brand "launches" by initially selling products to a few retailers. You're happy to get these sales, and seek more retailers to distribute your brand. At some point, a distributor or two might express interest in your brand, and you decide to let one or more do some hard work promoting your brand to channels that you don't know well.

In time, your brand becomes more popular, as more customers try out the product(s), seek to repurchase, and recommend to others. You might even have an online presence through your own account or one of your retailers.

Then the day comes that you discover—or you are notified by an upset brick-and-mortar retailer—that your brand is being sold on Amazon, and (typically) at a price much lower than you want. You're confused about this, as you never sold product to Amazon, or expressly told any retailer or distributor that they could sell on Amazon. And chances are some of the third-party sellers have company names you've never heard of from your sales team.

What is going on?

Diverted products (also known as grey-market product, or parallel-market products) are items that are sold by a retailer or distributor to another retailer outside of the intended market or channel.

For example, let's say your brand has contracted with a distributor to sell goods to brick-and-mortar retail stores, yet the distributor also quietly sells product to online retailers, counter to your brand's stated policies. While the sale is usually legal, it is generally not the intention of the brand or manufacturer to make product available to these additional retailers/resellers. As a result, the brand loses control of the distribution of its product.

The grey-market reseller can and typically will operate outside the control of the brand's reseller policies or pricing policies (e.g., Minimum Advertised Price/MAP or Manufacturer's Suggested Retail Price/MSRP). Thus with the loss of *distribution* control also comes the loss of *pricing* control—as well as control over how your brand is represented on Amazon to customers.

In the process your authorized resellers get upset, and it becomes increasingly difficult to recruit additional authorized resellers as the perceived value of your brand erodes.

In the U.S., the "First-Sale Doctrine" is a legal concept limiting what the rights-holder of a brand can do to control who re-sells its products. Essentially, the doctrine states that an individual can resell its legally purchased products to someone else. This applies to grey-market sellers if (a) the products are authentic, and (b) there is no material difference between the reseller's product and the brand's product.

There are hundreds of very sophisticated, well-financed grey-market sellers who know the tricks of the trade regarding how to source product to sell on the Amazon marketplace. While this business model can keep such resellers on their toes with constant cease-and-desist letters from frustrated brands, most of these resellers believe they can use the First-Sale Doctrine to continue their practices.

What Went Wrong?

What is it that's going awry when a brand's product is easily accessible to grey-market resellers?

Many brands believe they have airtight reseller policies to protect them from grey-market resellers. In reality, the brand's motives are rarely aligned with those of its authorized distributors or retailers.

The distributor/retailer usually is looking to make sales in the short run by turning inventory quickly to whomever will purchase, whereas the brand is usually willing to forgo some revenue and even profit today to protect and build its brand for the future. In other words, the brand *won't* necessarily sell to just anyone who's looking to buy—whereas the distributor/retailer will. Distributors/retailers generally aren't invested in brand reputation and position over the long haul, so they're more likely to make a sale if it involves making a quick buck.

If the quick sale is to a grey-market reseller that doesn't directly compete with the distributor/retailer (e.g., brick-and-mortar retailer grey-marketing product to an online reseller), there is even more incentive to make a quick sale of some inventory. This is usually a cash sale where the distributor/retailer makes an easy 2-5% profit margin—sometimes without the distributor even handling inventory, as the product is drop-shipped from the (unwitting) brand directly to the distributor's customer.

Some brands offer volume discounts to larger distributors/retailers, which implicitly creates opportunity for those distributors/retailers to make a few extra percentage points of margin by selling the product to a grey-market reseller. The distributor can afford to sell the product at a lower price, giving the grey-market reseller enough opportunity to still make its own margin.

If a brand doesn't carefully track all sales through every distributor, it becomes easier for a distributor to divert 10-20% of its inventory volume to grey-market resellers.

The sale of grey-market product tends to be a symptom of price volatility. If a brand can remove pricing discrepancies across markets or pricing volatility within a market, the incentive for distributors/retailers to cheat their brands will reduce significantly. Grey-market resellers will then pursue other brands that aren't paying as much attention to their price volatility.

Some common causes of price volatility include:

1. A brand offers *high-low pricing* (i.e., repeated large swings in prices on the same items) in the form of short-term discounted channel prices during certain times of the year. Distributors can stock up on inventory at such times, purportedly to sell over the coming months, but instead move inventory quickly to grey-market sellers.

2. A brand offers retailers the opportunity to discount significantly for short-term periods, enabling not only retailers but also well-financed consumers to load up on inventory they can resell at a later point at the higher, regular price.

3. A brand offers ongoing volume discounts, allowing distributors/retailers to place bigger orders that capitalize on the lower wholesale prices. Unlike short-term pricing discounts, larger distributors can take advantage of these lower wholesale prices any time of the year.

4. Differences between international and U.S. pricing caused by simple exchange rates or fluctuations in otherwise stable exchange rates create opportunities for distributors to re-import (parallel import) product from one (lower-priced)

country into another (higher-priced) country. We have seen situations where a brand seeks to expand its footprint into a new international market by offering lower initial prices in that market, only to find that those products end up back in the U.S. (because some international resellers made a good margin by re-selling this cheaply-acquired product back to U.S. sellers). Without an international pricing team to pay attention to such issues, it can be hard to figure out where these transactions originate.

5. Unusual channels like offshore oil rigs and duty-free shops are favorite channels for moving vast amounts of packaged consumer goods, because they involve less documentation and oversight than other distribution channels. This results in an ideal situation for diverting product.

6. Stolen product can be acquired quickly in bulk from the dishonest employees of retailers that do not have tight controls over inventory. Large national retailers might have an acceptable shrinkage target of, say, 2 percent of units. This seems small unless tens of thousands of units are being shipped across the retailer's national footprint. We have seen these stolen units landing in all sorts of hands, including Amazon Retail.

7. Returned products can create another channel in which oversight is poor and it's not always clear how many of the returned units are re-sellable or discarded. Pallets of returned products can easily be marked as discarded, when in fact they are quietly diverted for new-condition sale somewhere where they shouldn't be available. If product has already been written off by management, no one is going to investigate whether it really did end up being sent to the dump or recycled.

8. The brand's own sales department can be the source of the problem if they are rewarded for hitting sales goals without having to show exactly where all units ended up. Sales team members might make product available to grey-market resellers to meet quotas, even though they know that they aren't supposed to. With little oversight or tracking, there is little risk of being caught.

A conflict of interest is created when the brand executive's goals are to build and protect the brand over the long-term, while the sales team is incentivized for hitting short-term sales goals. To address this, senior leadership may need to step in and ensure that the sales team walk away from certain sales opportunities in order to protect the brand.

How Amazon Retail Participates in Grey-Market Channels

When Amazon Retail wants your brand, it will go to various extremes to locate inventory. Usually, the Amazon vendor managers start by calling the brand to identify the level of interest in setting up a first-party relationship. In some categories, such as Health, and for important product lines, Amazon Retail may offer to gate (i.e., restrict the sale of) the product's existing listings in exchange for the brand making Amazon Retail an exclusive/semi-exclusive retailer. As discussed earlier, this can be an appealing offer for brands that have already lost control of their distribution.

If a brand turns down Amazon Retail's offer to do business together, Amazon Retail may start scouring for distributors or retailers— domestic or international—that might be interested in sourcing the brand's product to Amazon Retail. Since Amazon Retail can make large dollar purchases without difficulty, this type of transaction may be appealing to a distributor or retailer that needs to hit its own quarterly numbers, especially if oversight from the brand is lax.

Essentially, Amazon Retail is willing to source the product of a brand it wants by any means necessary—and if the brand won't play ball, then Amazon Retail might source from grey-market sellers.

Further assisting Amazon Retail's cause are grey-market-creating distributors or retailers that set up Vendor Express accounts (https://vendorexpress.amazon.com) to make products available to wholesale to Amazon Retail. If any of their inventory UPC-matches any products that Amazon Retail is also pursuing, Amazon Retail's computers can automatically start placing purchase orders from these distributors or retailers, without much human vendor manager involvement (making it even easier for grey-market providers to go undetected by anyone inside Amazon asking questions about the source of products). Furthermore, Amazon rarely reveals to brands the names of the companies supplying product to Amazon through Vendor Express.

Amazon Retail isn't always doing adequate due diligence regarding the sources of Vendor Express products, so both diverted and stolen inventory can find its way into Amazon Retail's inventory by way of these Vendor Express first-party sellers. If a brand doesn't have adequate control of its distribution network, it is easy for distributors to divert sizeable quantities of inventory directly to Amazon Retail via such accounts. Since Amazon Retail won't divulge the source of its products, it can be very difficult for brands to prevent this means of product access.

Two precautionary notes for brands to consider: first, we have seen Amazon Retail not only source diverted product, much to a brand's chagrin—but further, tell the brand that it will *continue* sourcing like this until the brand finally agrees to wholesale directly to Amazon Retail. (Yes, this is essentially blackmail.) Given that Amazon will not get involved in helping to manage distribution for a brand, it's unfortunate that Amazon Retail itself can be one of the biggest culprits in selling diverted product.

Second, even when Amazon Retail *is* already sourcing directly from a brand, it may also discreetly supplement additional units of the same brand from grey-market sources to ensure adequate levels of high-demand inventory. One of our clients was stunned when an Amazon vendor manager assured the client that he was only sourcing product directly from the brand—even though sales data clearly indicated that Amazon Retail was selling far more units than it was buying.

Ten Meaningful Ways to Limit Product Diversion

For a grey-market product to be interesting to a reseller, two conditions typically need to be present:

    a. a meaningful margin opportunity, and
    b. few roadblocks to selling that product quickly

If the margins simply aren't there to support multiple levels of reselling, then the grey-market reseller will move on to a brand where such reselling offers better margin incentive.

If there are too many obstacles to the grey-market seller's ability to move product quickly and discreetly, the seller will likewise pursue a brand where the sale is less risky as well as more lucrative.

We are reminded of the story of gazelles on the plains of Tanzania: a gazelle doesn't have to be the fastest to escape the hungry lion; it simply must avoid being the slowest. The brand that puts up at least some resistance to the grey-market seller will be much less appealing than the thousands of other brands that don't. "Putting up resistance" in this case means securing product distribution on the Amazon marketplace, and monitoring what's going on in the channel.

Here's what a brand can do to make its product less appealing to grey-market sellers:

1. **Offer different prices to different channels**. If companies in one channel are consistently responsible for large amounts of diverted product, the brand has the legal right to charge higher wholesale prices for its products sold through that channel. This action reduces the financial incentive for the diverter to continue. One word of caution: too large a difference in wholesale pricing between different channels could lead to new forms of cross-channel diversion.

2. **Create reseller policies that clearly outline your rules — and the consequences of not following your rules.** To avoid potential anti-trust litigation and other liabilities, roll out these reseller policies unilaterally so they are not contracts between the brand and the reseller. Get your distributors and resellers to sign that they have received the reseller policy, not that they agree to the terms.

3. **Create and enforce policies related to Minimum Advertised Price or Minimum Resale Price**. Again, these should not be contracts, but rather unilaterally communicated policies. Enforcement is critical to show distributors and retailers are paying attention. If you catch someone breaking the rules and decide to drop them as a distributor or retailer, make sure that word gets out so everyone knows you are serious.

4. **Where realistic, offer manufacturer warranties with your products**. You can make these warranties available only on products purchased from authorized resellers. As trademark attorneys have emphasized to us, the authorized seller's warranty versus the unauthorized seller's lack of a warranty does, in fact, constitute a material difference in the products. Material differences can mean trademark infringement, and Amazon will usually act on a complaint related to a trademark infringement. If you put your brand's warranty information and list of authorized resellers up on

your own brand site, it's easier for customers and retailers (authorized and unauthorized alike) to see.

5. **If applicable, offer post-sale customer service only for customers who purchase authorized product from authorized sellers.** While customers may get upset when a brand doesn't honor what they believed to be a legitimate product purchase, customers rarely make this mistake twice. Again, post your list of authorized resellers on your own site, so customers can see who they are.

6. **Where appropriate, introduce storage or handling guidelines for your products.** Because you cannot validate whether unauthorized sellers are following your brand's guidelines (such as temperature-controlled transport or storage), this will give you legal precedent to file complaints with Amazon by seeking the removal of such sellers' products if they do not comply with storage and handling guidelines.

7. **Work on getting your brand gated/restricted on Amazon.** This isn't common knowledge, but Amazon will gate product listings if a brand can demonstrate that there are customer safety issues if the product is purchased from anyone other than an authorized reseller. You may have to get a little creative here, but if the product goes on the skin or inside the body, it's easier to convince Amazon that you can't guarantee safety to Amazon customers when products are purchased from grey-market sellers.

8. **On your brand website, list your *authorized* resellers for all customers and retailers to see.** As mentioned in points 4 and 5 above, this will help with ensuring that only customers who purchase from authorized sellers get your warranties and customer service. Customers want those benefits and will therefore look for authorized sellers — and avoid grey-market ones — if you make this clear and make the authorized sellers

easy to find. It also shows grey-market sellers you're keeping an eye on what's going on in the channel. (Your authorized sellers will appreciate it too!) Even if you are the only authorized reseller of the product, list this information on your brand website.

9. **Consider putting serial numbers or batch numbers on your products**. Tie these numbers back to specific distributors/retailers. When you test-buy unauthorized resellers' products, you can easily identify the source of the product, making it easier to take action (with visual data) and close leaky channels.

   Furthermore, if a grey-market reseller chooses to remove the serial numbers or batch numbers, this qualifies as a material alteration of your product, and likely constitutes infringement. In any case, Amazon doesn't tolerate such alterations, and will work with a brand that can demonstrate this sort of modification. Finally, once you have serial numbers and batch numbers in place (whether you make the marking discrete or obvious), it's worth letting your channels know that you have started tracking products to specific channels, thereby reducing the likelihood that a distributor will even try large-scale diverting.

10. **Control your returns process more closely**. That means not only customer returns, but distributor returns and lots that failed initial production testing. Know who's testing your products, and what happens to products that are deemed un-resalable. Do spot checks to make sure that these un-resalable products *really* aren't re-sellable—and that they're not being diverted somewhere else. Keep track of how many units come into returns, and where each unit ultimately ends up. Too many brands overlook what happens with their returns. This laxity can allow thousands of returned units to get moved into the arms of opportunists.

How Brands Can Effectively Challenge the First-Sale Doctrine

There are legitimate ways to get unauthorized resellers removed from Amazon. The best long-term solution is to shut off product access for these sellers in the first place, through some of the methods mentioned earlier. But it's also appropriate for brands to file Amazon Infringement tickets if the brands can show that the products being sold by the grey-market resellers/unauthorized resellers are somehow materially different from the authorized units.

Appropriate cause for attention from Amazon's Infringement team includes material differences caused by repackaging, removal of serial numbers or batch IDs, modification of UPCs, removal of warranties or instruction manuals, units not meant for individual sale, or foreign-language units being combined with domestic language units. Typically, the brand will be required to verify the quality issue by providing Amazon with an order number from a test buy, as well as a clear explanation of where the material difference can be found.

While we are not trademark lawyers, we have seen many situations in which such modifications can be convincingly positioned as trademark violations, which makes any offer to sell such grey-market units an illegal activity trumping any First-Sale Doctrine. We advise that brands confer with trademark attorneys who specialize in online channels (e.g., http://vorys.com, https://www.genericlaw.com, http://www.theprivatelabellawyer.com).

Summary

The Amazon marketplace is an efficient place for companies to quickly sell lower-priced units of desirable brands if they can obtain them. They often do it under the guise of an anonymous Vendor Express account or a Doing Business As (DBA) third-party seller name. The more diverted product that a brand allows to leak out, the tougher time it will have controlling its pricing, brand content, selection, and inventory levels on Amazon. These issues will have negative repercussions for their relationships with the brick-and-mortar retailers who are following the brand's distribution rules.

Amazon Retail itself can be one of the culprits—finding and selling grey-market product on Amazon through Vendor Express —often unbeknownst to the brand.

While no single approach to limiting or removing grey-market sellers will work consistently, the most successful brands are those that keep an eye on their so-called "biggest and best" distributors and retailers, while proactively reminding their authorized channels of authorized resale policies, and the consequences of not following those policies.

CONCLUSION

The brand that cleans its Amazon channel of unauthorized sellers and diverted product, while ensuring that it is represented by complete and accurate content on its Amazon product listings, is setting a solid foundation for growth on the Amazon marketplace.

However, the brand will still require constant nurturing through marketing and regularly refreshed SEO, along with continuous oversight to ensure that the catalog remains free of inaccurate or inappropriate product listings.

As challenging as the Amazon marketplace can be with its own procedures and policies, the rewards of selling on Amazon can be significant when the brand is in control of its presence there. It's imperative that a brand understands and manages this channel's direct and indirect impact on its overall distribution strategy. But with a solid foundation and adequate maintenance, Amazon can play a valuable role in a brand's presence and profit.

GLOSSARY

"Add to Cart" button / Buy Box / Buy Box algorithm: When a customer looks at a product page on Amazon, they can add the item to the shopping cart by clicking the "Add to Cart" button. Because there are often many sellers competing for the sale on the same item, Amazon has come up with an algorithm that selects the default seller whose product will be added when the customer clicks the "Add to Cart" button. This algorithm is called the "Buy Box algorithm", and determines:

- which sellers are eligible to be the "Buy Box winner" and
- which eligible seller at any given time is the winner.

Amazon prioritizes sellers with a minimum sales history (at least 30 days of sales history in a particular category), high performance metrics (including low order cancellation rate, high rate of on-time fulfillment with a confirmation sent to customers, strong customer feedback, and other metrics), and pricing that does not exceed the known list price. When sellers meet these criteria, they become eligible to win the Buy Box. If there are multiple eligible sellers on the same product listings, Amazon usually rotates these as the "Buy Box winner." Using Amazon's Fulfillment by Amazon (FBA) program greatly improves a seller's Buy Box eligibility.

Sellers seeking to grow their businesses must understand what it takes to be the "Buy-Box-winning" seller because, unfortunately, a low price is not enough.

Some recent research by service provider Feedvisor (*Buy Box Bible*, 2016 edition) indicated that the key variables impacting a seller's ability to win the Buy Box, in order, are:

1. Fulfillment method (fulfillment by Amazon is better than fulfillment by merchant)

2. Landed price (product price + shipping cost = landed price; the lower the landed price, the more likely a seller is to win the buy box)
3. Seller rating (if a seller has strong performance metrics, it is more likely to win the Buy Box than a seller whose metrics are floundering — performance metrics include on-time delivery, cancellation rate, customer service response time, etc.)
4. **Shipping time** (the faster the product gets to customers, the better; if sellers are doing the shipping themselves, and taking 10-14 days, that hurts the seller's ability to win the Buy Box relative to a seller that uses FBA, which ships and delivers within 2 days)

Amazon Seller (third-party sellers, Amazon Retail): On Amazon, there are two types of sellers: Amazon Retail (also known as "first-party" or 1P), and everyone else. The Amazon company has a buying team that sources product directly from manufacturers, and offers those items for sale on Amazon. Meanwhile, more than two million other sellers also offer their products for sale on Amazon. These other sellers are called "third-party" or 3P sellers. They make up the overwhelming majority of product selection on Amazon, and about half of the sales volume and revenue on Amazon.

Amazon Marketing Services (AMS): This is the Amazon advertising portal for companies selling product to Amazon Retail. Unlike third-party Sponsored Product Ads (see definition later in this section), which is for third-party sellers, the AMS portal offers several advertising options, including *Headline Search* (banner ads at the top of search results), *Product Display* (ads on competitors' product detail pages), and *Sponsored Products.* (The first-party Sponsored Products options are similar but not identical to third-party Sponsored Product Ads; a third-party seller's Sponsored Product ad shows up only when the seller is the Buy Box winner, whereas a first-party

Sponsored Product ad shows up regardless of who the Buy Box winning seller is.)

To access AMS, a company must have either an active Vendor Central or Vendor Express account with Amazon retail.

Amazon Marketing Group (AMG): Designed to help brands create broad brand awareness on Amazon, this platform offers brands the opportunity to buy display ads, mobile banner ads, mobile interstitial ads, image and text ads, in-stream video ads, and Kindle advertising. Typically, brands using the AMG program will end up spending at least $35,000, making this set of advertising tools less relevant for small or medium-sized brands selling on Amazon. The advertising is primarily focused on brand building; it is not as obvious whether and how these efforts immediately drive sales on Amazon.

ASIN: This is an acronym for "Amazon Standard Identification Number." It's the unique 10-digit product identifier assigned to a product when it is listed for the first time on Amazon. It is usually tied to a product's unique UPC (Universal Product Code), or EAN (also known as the International Article Number—basically the European equivalent of a UPC). You may hear the term "BOO" number as well, because the structure of the ASIN typically begins with B-zero-zero, followed by seven letters and numbers. If the item is a book, the item's ASIN is in fact the book's unique 10-digit International Standard Book Number, or ISBN. Once an ASIN is created, it isn't tied to any specific seller. It identifies only the product, not the sellers of the product.

Brand Registry: A program for sellers who manufacture or sell their own branded products. The program's goal is to make it easier for sellers to manage their own brands and list their products on Amazon.com. Registering your brand with Amazon gives you increased control over your products' titles, details, bullet points, product description, meta-data, and other attributes. This program also gives you the ability to list products without UPCs or EANs, as in a case where you make customized items that don't have UPCs or EANs. A brand that submits its product information through the Brand Registry program can "lock down" the content used for its listings, so that other third-party sellers cannot change it or use inferior quality content that could harm the brand's reputation.

Cease and Desist Letter: In the context of the Amazon marketplace, the use of "C&D letters" is primarily a tool for brands to communicate to sellers that they must stop selling the brand on Amazon. Brands/trademark owners often consider it a trademark violation or other policy violation when an unauthorized seller offers the brand's products on Amazon. The effectiveness of cease and desist letters is inconsistent on Amazon, as many sellers completely ignore them. Nonetheless, we find multiple mailings of C&D letters to sellers will result in 60-80% of the sellers leaving the listings after 2 mailings. Upon receiving such letters, many sellers will stop selling the brand on Amazon, choosing to avoid any potential future legal action. While some sellers view these letters as a form of intimidation, brands see them as initial warnings. It is important to understand that Amazon is generally not interested in addressing unauthorized distribution issues, leaving such issues up to the brand to self-manage.

Counterfeit: In the context of the Amazon marketplace, counterfeit refers to items that are fake replicas of a trademarked brand. As such, the rightful brand owner has a legal right to protect its brand, and can file suit against the seller, or file an infringement complaint with Amazon. Typically, Amazon will ask for extensive proof that an item is counterfeit. But if a seller *is* proven to be selling counterfeits, the punishment by Amazon typically involves suspending or terminating the seller's account.

Recently, Amazon has had to deal with a significant increase in counterfeit products from overseas sellers flooding certain product categories with high-quality knockoffs. Amazon's inability to keep up with regulating and removing counterfeits has led to high-publicity brand defections from Amazon. While Amazon is typically responsive to counterfeit claims by customers or brands, the lag time to gather enough evidence to file a counterfeit claim is long enough that some professional counterfeiters have successfully made two to four weeks of sales before being kicked off the site. They will often reappear as new sellers under different seller names for additional rounds of two to four weeks of sales.

Customer Conversion: This metric defines that proportion of visitors to an Amazon product detail page who buy the product within a 24-hour period. If 100 people visit a product detail page, and 10 of them buy the product within the next 24 hours, the customer conversion rate is 10%. This metric is an important variable for determining which items show up at the top of Search results when customers look for items on Amazon.

Fulfillment by Amazon (FBA): Amazon offers a fee-based order fulfillment service for sellers called "Fulfillment by Amazon" or "FBA." Through this service, sellers send products in bulk to Amazon fulfillment centers, where Amazon then handles the preparation and shipping of individual customer orders. Amazon also handles product storage and customer returns for FBA orders. Because FBA orders are made available for Prime Shipping and Super Saver Shipping to Amazon customers, this program has become strategically critical to the success of most sellers on Amazon.

Gated Categories: Not all categories on Amazon are open to every seller. Some categories require permission from Amazon. Before you register on Amazon, it is important to check Seller Central to learn which categories are gated, and figure out if your items fall into those categories. If your items are in gated categories, you will want to read the instructions in Seller Central on how to apply to get "ungated" for those categories. If you're looking to sell items primarily in gated categories on Amazon, you will need to start the ungating request process immediately after registration. Be aware that asking to be ungated does not guarantee you will be granted permission, so you may find that Amazon isn't available to you as a sales channel.

Grey-market seller: These are typically sellers that sell product through channels not intended or authorized by the brand/trademark owners. For example, if a brand has a reseller policy stating that no one can sell the brand on Amazon, yet the product ends up being sold on Amazon, those sellers offering the product are most likely grey-market sellers. Grey-market sellers typically have sourced the product from distributors or retailers that "diverted" the product from intended channels to unintended channels.

Brands often develop online reseller policies with anti-diversion terms, specifically aimed at better controlling which resellers do and don't offer the brand's products on the Amazon marketplace. Unfortunately, without batch IDs, serial numbers or other tracking mechanisms, it is often an arduous battle to figure out who diverted product that ended up on Amazon. As Amazon rarely provides information to brands on the identity of sellers, it can be near impossible for brands to close these distribution loopholes that cause product to end up on Amazon.

MAP/MSRP/MRP: Minimum Advertised Price/ Manufacturer's Suggested Retail Price / Minimum Retail Price—these are three different mechanisms brands/manufacturers use to manage the price points at which their products are sold to customers. While there are different legal aspects to each, it is important to understand that brands/manufacturers use price as a method of defining the quality of their products. Consistent pricing across channels helps a brand create a reliable perception of the worth or value of the product. Brands that do not have such mechanisms (or are not effective at managing them) are often viewed as lower-quality by shoppers; customers know they can "shop around" to find the lowest price on that product.

Marketplace: The marketplace is simply the term used to describe the whole market of Amazon, including Amazon Retail, third-party sellers, and the customers all interacting on the Amazon.com shopping site.

Merchant-Fulfilled Network (MFN): This denotes that an Amazon seller fulfills an individual order itself. Very small sellers often fulfill from home, packing individual orders on their kitchen tables one at a time, printing shipping labels from their home printers, taking the orders to the Post Office/UPS/FedEx/DHL on a daily basis, and then confirming their shipments on Amazon (with a confirmation number from the shipping carrier — and this confirmation is important, as Amazon only pays sellers once the shipping confirmation has been shared with Amazon). These sellers are likely buying packing materials in bulk, and storing them in small nearby warehouses, their basements or their garages. For a small seller with few SKUs and few daily orders, this fulfillment process is manageable. A larger seller will need a warehouse or third-party (3PL) logistics partner to make large-scale MFN Orders feasible.

"Offer" Versus "Listing" Versus "Product Detail Page": A product must have a product detail page to appear for sale in Amazon's catalog. This is the page a customer sees when shopping, including a product title, bullet points, product description, images, etc. If a product does not yet have a product detail page in Amazon's catalog, then when the first seller indicates that it has that product for sale, Amazon will create a product catalog listing (a.k.a. "listing") and assigns a unique ASIN. The listing will contain the data content submitted by this first seller. The specific seller is said to have an "offer" on the listing, including the condition of the product for sale (e.g., "new", "used", etc.) and the pricing that the seller is using. As other sellers later indicate that they too have the same product to sell, each seller will add its "offer" to the existing listing (complete with information on the product condition and pricing to be used). Confusing the matter, some sellers may be able to change the original content on the listing because Amazon judges their content to be better than the content already submitted by prior sellers. If this happens, that specific seller's content will now be used to display to customers, instead as the default content on the product detail page.

A listing has its own ASIN, but many offers may exist on a listing. This one-listing-per-SKU model has helped create an easier shopping experience for customers, where they can see every seller's offer on a single product listing page, rather than having to look at many practically identical product listing pages (e.g., the current eBay model, where there is only 1 seller per product listing page – this model can be confusing for customers who wonder what the differences are across these seemingly identical listings).

Prime / Prime-Eligible: Amazon Prime is a shipping subscription program available to Amazon customers. For an annual $99 charge, Amazon customers get unlimited two-day shipping on products that are "Prime-eligible." Almost all items sold by Amazon Retail, and products sold by third-party sellers using the Fulfillment by Amazon program are Prime-eligible. While the Amazon Prime membership also includes access to other features (like certain Amazon video and Kindle content), this program is primarily a shipping program that has driven customer loyalty to levels where Amazon Prime customers now outspend non-Prime customers more than two to one each year. With an estimated 60 million+ customers using the Amazon Prime program as of July 2016, this program has developed into one of the most important drivers of Amazon marketplace growth.

When Amazon Prime customers are signed into the Amazon site, their product search results will heavily favor Prime Eligible offers. Thanks to their higher search results, these items will usually receive a disproportionate share of customer traffic, as well as much higher customer conversion rates than non-Prime products.

Product Detail Page: The Product Detail page, or product page, is the visual representation of a single product listing on Amazon. On this page, a customer can see the title, brand name, bullet points, product description, price, shipping time frame and sellers offering this item. By consolidating this information, Amazon has made the shopping experience easier for customers and competing sellers alike. As a seller, it is important to learn what it takes to manage the accuracy and completeness of content on the product detail page so that customers have enough information to decide whether to buy the item.

Product Diversion: see *Grey-Market Seller.*

Product Review Groups: There are a number of public and private groups of people who will review products for Amazon sellers. These product review groups typically request access to purchase product at a heavy discount (40-99% off normal price), with the expectation that the members of the group purchasing these products will leave an honest review for the seller.

As Amazon has cracked down on review groups that are not following Amazon's Terms of Service (TOS) regarding how product reviews can be sought and fulfilled, Amazon has also evolved how it grades different product reviews. As of early Q1-2016, we have seen that the size of the discount offered to product review groups determines whether Amazon classifies the product review as a "verified" or "unverified" product review. Based on our observation, product reviews from purchases generated by coupon codes offering 40-45% or more off the regular price tend to be classified as "unverified," whereas less-discounted product generates "verified" discounts. This distinction is important, as verified product reviews are weighted more heavily by Amazon in the search algorithm.

Retail Arbitrage: This is a business model in which products for online resale are sourced by buying the products as a consumer from local stores (rather than buying products from manufacturers or distributors). If local stores offer short-term sale prices on products, it can be possible to acquire product as a consumer and resell with enough margin to make a profit on Amazon as a reseller, even after Amazon selling commissions and fulfillment fees.

While the margin percentage can be attractive, sellers will struggle to build such a business to a very large size without the benefit of sophisticated software and extensive human support to acquire product across dozens of stores. In our experience, the few large and profitable retail arbitrage sellers invest in storage facilities to hold inventory from one low-demand time of year to be sold at a higher-demand of year (e.g., toys and holiday decorations sold at clearance prices in January, to be sold the next November or December).

Stale Inventory: Inventory that goes unsold for extensive periods of time can be classified as stale inventory. While not obsolete, it can become inventory that is not expected to sell without the benefit of clearance prices. Sellers with a handle on inventory management proactively review their inventory each month to make sure that it doesn't become stale, and will slowly discount inventory before it reaches the point that it becomes incredibly difficult to sell (e.g., trying to sell electronics/personal computer models that are three years old, when new models are being launched every three to six months).

If sellers are using FBA to store their inventory, Amazon storage fees will help to remind sellers that inventory isn't meant to get stale in Amazon's fulfillment centers. In fact, after six months, Amazon increases the storage fees on most items by a factor of nearly ten-fold, as a less-than-subtle nudge to get sellers to move stale inventory out of the fulfillment centers.

Seller Central: This is the portal that every third-party seller uses to see its inventory, sales, order fulfillment, customer inquiries/feedback, and payment disbursement information.

Seller Performance: This is the Amazon organization that is responsible for patrolling and regulating the marketplace. They act as the police, judge and jury on appropriate and inappropriate seller behavior, ranging from what proportion of each seller's orders are being shipped on time, to customer complaints about counterfeit products, to seller notifications about changing regulations on the marketplace. Most sellers know Seller Performance as the organization that sends them warnings for policy violations when they break rules.

While there are several people that work on the Seller Performance team, the team also has extensive software support for tracking sellers, emails and transactions at all times. Because communication between this organization and sellers happens almost exclusively through email, many sellers complain that the organization is mysterious, and does not help sellers understand the root causes of issues that arise with their accounts.

Seller SKU: The Seller SKU is the unique code that the seller uses in its Amazon catalog to label its offer on a specific product (associated with an ASIN) in a specific condition. The seller can create any unique code it wants for each offer; there is no specified or required naming convention. The seller can have different Seller SKUs on the same product/ASIN if the seller is listing multiple units of a product in different condition. For example, if the seller had a new-condition offer and a used-condition offer for the same ASIN, the seller would create two separate seller SKUs to differentiate these two offers. Likewise, if the seller chose to list one offer for sale through Amazon's Fulfillment by Amazon (or FBA) program, and another offer for sale to be fulfilled by the seller, those two offers would also get separate SKUs in the seller's Amazon catalog.

Note that only the seller sees information on the Seller SKU details— it's basically an internal bookkeeping mechanism to help the seller keep track of its offers on Amazon.

Seller Support: This is the organization that provides email, phone, and chat support for sellers seeking answers to questions about their business on Amazon.

SEO on Amazon: Search Engine Optimization (SEO) on Amazon is the process sellers use to create detailed product listings employing the optimal combination and placement of terms that match those customers use to search desired products. When a seller invests time to develop product listings emphasizing the right titles, bullet points, images, product feedback, product descriptions, answered questions and keywords (meta-data), this effort should pay off in increased visibility for those products. In addition, offering products through FBA is a form of SEO that yields a bump in search engine placement.

With over 300 million products in the Amazon catalog, it is critical that products effectively capture the terms and phrases that customers most associate with the items, and therefore use when searching for them. For example, if searching for novelty socks with monkeys on them, a customer is likely to search for "novelty socks" or "socks with monkeys" or "monkey socks" — all terms that could suitably be incorporated in the key product characteristics for that listing.

Unfortunately, far too many Amazon product listings are hastily created, or never refreshed to reflect ever-changing customer preferences for terms that are relevant to the products they represent. Products with slapdash or dated listings are less likely to be discovered by Amazon customers.

Sponsored Product Ads: Third-party "Sponsored Products" (or "Sponsored Product Ads") is a pay-per-click marketing tool in Seller Central that allows third-party sellers to promote their products on Amazon. Through either manual targeting (where a seller identifies a specific list of keywords that it wants to bid on) or automatic targeting (where Amazon picks the words base on its own algorithms for what it believes are optimal terms), the seller can bid for placement on search results from customers. If a customer is searching Amazon for "blue socks," and the seller has chosen to bid on "blue socks," then the seller will show up in the search results. How high on the list the seller shows up is based on how much the seller bid per click. If the seller bid enough, the product may show up at the top of the search results, labeled as a "sponsored" search result – essentially, an ad. However, it's vital to be aware that no matter how much you bid, *your ad will only show up in search results if you're currently the Buy Box winner on that product.* When a customer clicks on a Sponsored Product ad, they are sent directly to your product detail page.

This type of marketing is ideal for a product that doesn't yet have the traffic, customer conversion, and/or sales to bring it organically to the top of search results when a customer searches for related terms.

Third-party sellers in over 30 categories ranging from Electronics to Health & Beauty can use Sponsored Ads to augment organic traffic they already receive. Adult products, used products, and products in closed (gated) categories, however, are not eligible for Sponsored Products Ads.

Sponsored Products can also be set up in Amazon Marketing Services (AMS) on the first-party side. (See *AMS*.) The functionality is basically the same, except that with third-party Sponsored Product ads, the seller must be the Buy Box winner to have its ads surface. On the first-party side, a Sponsored Product ad can show up independent of whether Amazon Retail or a third-party seller is the Buy Box winner.

Tax Nexus: As Benjamin Franklin said, "In this world nothing can be said to be certain, except death and taxes." Selling on Amazon is no different—there are tax implications to any selling you do here. What is tax nexus? The responsibility you may have to collect or pay tax based on a state in which you have a sales presence. While we certainly aren't tax accountants and encourage you to talk with your own tax accountant, it's important to understand that you will need to provide Amazon with your reseller tax ID number as part of your registration process. And if you choose to collect state tax in specific states, you will want to enter your tax ID numbers into Seller Central to enable Amazon to collect the sales tax on your behalf. While Amazon can help you collect tax on customer orders, you alone are responsible for paying your taxes.

Vendor Express: Accessible through vendorexpress.amazon.com, this is a self-service portal for anyone to offer products for sale to Amazon Retail. The seller enters into the portal information on what products it is offering, the asking price and the quantities available. Then Amazon Retail's computers determine if these products are of interest to Amazon Retail. While Amazon Retail already has another portal called Vendor Central, that is by invitation only, and typically managed by Amazon vendor managers instead of Amazon computers.

We discuss Vendor Express specifically because it has become a channel through which Amazon Retail is able to access vast quantities of grey market product – product that brands don't want Amazon Retail to access are now offered to Amazon Retail by grey market sellers and distributors. As the selling of products through Vendor Express can be done without the knowledge of the brands, this portal enables Amazon Retail to access huge amounts of product selection without the permission of brands, thereby creating significant distribution headaches for brands trying to figure out how Amazon Retail got their products to sell on Amazon.

Company Overview

Buy Box Experts (www.buyboxexperts.com) is a managed account services agency. Our clients are brands looking to sell their products on the Amazon marketplace strategically and successfully, and needing clarity on the distribution model that optimizes their strategic needs, and the support to execute that model.

Our firm helps brands control and manage key levers (e.g., branding, pricing, distribution, catalog selection, inventory levels, advertising) to create a profitable, online business starting with the Amazon marketplace. For most clients, Buy Box Experts provides day-to-day management of a client's Amazon channel business, bringing best-practice experience and techniques to:

- Inventory management and forecasting
- Listing creation and SEO optimization
- Catalog cleanup of existing listings
- Channel cleanup and brand protection
- Online advertising program management
- Customer service
- Product reviews and feedback
- Multi-channel account management on US and international Amazon channels

If your brand is seeking guidance on how to optimize the Amazon channel as part of your overall distribution strategy, let's talk.

James Thomson, Ph.D.
Partner
james@buyboxexperts.com
(801) 893-3689 phone

Joseph Hansen
Founding Partner
joseph@buyboxexperts.com
(801) 900-5140 phone

Author Biographies

James Thomson was formerly head of Amazon Services, the division of Amazon responsible for recruiting tens of thousands of sellers annually to the Amazon marketplace. He also served as the first Fulfillment by Amazon (FBA) account manager. Prior to Amazon, James was a management consultant and banker.

He holds a Bachelor of Science from University of Alberta, an MBA from Vanderbilt University (Owen School), and a Ph.D. in Marketing (B2B Pricing and Distribution) from Northwestern University (Kellogg School). James has published or contributed to more than 20 articles and podcasts on e-commerce issues, and guest lectured at more than a dozen top business schools around the world.

Joseph Hansen is a seasoned entrepreneur and ecommerce expert. He has founded and sold four brand companies that used the Amazon channel. In 2012, Hansen founded Buy Box Experts, a consultancy supporting brands on Amazon.

Buy Box Experts provides full service account management to help organizations entirely outsource the day-to-day operations of their marketplace channels. The company also helps management teams to control online brand equity, stabilize pricing, and improve product sales and marketing. By developing an innovative Marketplace Optimization strategy for e-retailers, Joseph has created an invaluable toolkit for those looking to grow and control their e-commerce operations. He holds a Bachelor's degree in Exercise Science from Brigham Young University.

In 2015, James and Joseph co-founded the PROSPER Show (prospershow.com), a continuing education conference for large Amazon sellers.